Bible Crosswords

Collection #2

Compiled and Edited
by *Toni Sortor*

A Barbour Book

Bible Crosswords Collection #2
Copyright © MCMXCIV by Barbour and Company, Inc.
All rights reserved.
Printed in the United States of America.
Published by Barbour and Company, Inc.
P.O. Box 719
Uhrichsville, OH 44683
ISBN 1-55748-595-X

96 97 98 99 5 4

Bible
Crosswords

Collection #2

PUZZLE 1

Evelyn Boyington

ACROSS CLUES

1. Look _____ new heavens and a new earth. (2 Pet. 3:13)
4. I will _____ thee: on the third day. (2 Kgs. 20:5)
8. Health resorts.
12. My days _____ like a shadow. (Ps. 102:11)
13. Enter _____ his gates with thanksgiving. (Ps. 100:4)
14. We have seen his star in the _____. (Matt. 2:2)
15. I will destroy this _____. (Mark 14:58)
17. _____ no man any thing. (Rom. 13:8)
19. A greeting.
20. To hurt.
21. We _____ great plainness of speech. (2 Cor. 3:12)
22. He _____ to meet them. (Gen. 18:2)
23. A narrow cut.
25. Voice of _____ crying in the wilderness. (Matt. 3:3)
26. With _____ life will I satisfy him. (Ps. 91:16)
27. An _____ of oil for an ephah. (Ezek. 45:24)
28. I saw thee under the _____ tree. (John 1:50)
29. Arise, take up thy _____. (Matt. 9:6)
30. What think _____ of Christ? (Matt. 22:42)
31. We were _____ of God to be put in trust. (1 Thes. 2:4)
33. Chemical symbol for radium.
35. Hear my _____, O God. (Ps. 61:1)
36. Thou shalt _____ about thee. (Job 11:18)
37. Babylon is taken, _____ is confounded. (Jer. 50:2)
38. O Lord, _____ shall I say! (Josh. 7:8)
40. Height (abbr.).
41. He moveth his _____ like a cedar. (Job 40:17)

42. Even as a _____ gathereth her chickens. (Matt. 23:37)
43. Not willing that _____ should perish. (2 Pet. 3:9)
44. I would thou wert cold or _____. (Rev. 3:15)
45. A piece (abbr.).
46. Wheat beard.
47. _____ and built up in him. (Col. 2:7)
50. The high places also of _____. (Hosea 10:8)
52. The children of _____ of Hezekiah. (Ezra 2:16)
54. _____ up for yourselves treasures in heaven. (Matt. 6:20)
55. An examination.
56. Gaddiel the son of _____. (Num. 13:10)
57. How long will it be _____ thou be quiet? (Jer. 47:6)

DOWN CLUES

1. Liberal soul shall be made _____. (Prov. 11:25)
2. Raw metal.
3. My joy might _____ in you. (John 15:11)
4. Every mountain and _____ shall be brought low. (Luke 3:5)
5. Compass point.
6. Marvel not _____ this. (John 5:28)
7. _____ thy shoe from off thy foot. (Josh. 5:15)
8. Whereas I was blind, now I _____. (John 9:25)
9. Dad.
10. Ain, Remmon, and Ether, and _____. (Josh. 19:7)
11. O death, where is thy _____? (1 Cor. 15:55)
16. Brought me up also out of an horrible _____. (Ps. 40:2)
18. _____ are the children of God. (Rom. 8:16)
21. Christ died for the _____. (Rom. 5:6)
22. Moses took the _____ of God in his hand. (Ex. 4:20)
23. Timid.
24. I will _____ with my fathers. (Gen. 47:30)

4

25. An horn of _____. (1 Kgs. 1:39)
26. The Lord _____ me. (Gen. 24:27)
28. For then would I _____ away. (Ps. 55:6)
29. Therefore shall he _____ in harvest. (Prov. 20:4)
31. Thou _____ the Son of God. (John 1:49)
32. Powers of thinking.
33. Shimei and _____, and the mighty men. (1 Kgs. 1:8)
34. The Lord is good to _____. (Ps. 145:9)
35. How _____ these things be? (John 3:9)
37. The Lord mighty in _____. (Ps. 24:8)
38. Sowed tares among the _____. (Matt. 13:25)

39. The first of your dough for an _____ offering. (Num. 15:20)
40. And led Him away to _____ first. (John 18:13)
41. Ye take _____ much upon you. (Num. 16:3)
43. A sound of sympathy.
44. The sons of Lotan; _____, and Homam. (1 Chron. 1:39)
46. Go to the ____, thou sluggard. (Prov. 6:6)
47. The Lord dried up the water of the _____ sea. (Josh 2:10)
48. Give _____ to my words. (Ps. 5:1)
49. A solution for coloring.
51. Suffix used in forming plurals.
53. Peace _____ him that is far off. (Isa. 57:19)

5

PUZZLE 2

Helen Walter

ACROSS CLUES

1. Garden of _____.
5. Wander.
8. He is of _____; ask him. (John 9:21)
11. And the _____ and the morning were the first day. (Gen. 1:5)
12. The first man.
13. The first woman.
14. Pare.
16. Doctor (abbr.).
17. Director (abbr.).
19. Grass.
21. This _____ in remembrance of me. (Luke 22:19)
23. Lands surrounded by water.
26. Make broader.
28. Day and night shall not _____. (Gen. 8:22)
29. Chicago transportation.
31. What hast thou _____? (Gen. 4:10)
32. Spelling (abbr.).
33. Ye shall not eat of every _____ of the garden? (Gen 3:1)
35. Old Testament (abbr.).
36. Naomi's daughter-in-law. (Ruth 1:4)
37. Relatives. Kin?
40. Son of Adam and Eve.
41. _____ shall not eat of it. (Gen. 3:3)
42. Let _____ make man. (Gen. 1:26)
44. Hear the word of God, and _____ it. (Luke 8:21)
45. Vase.
47. Naked.
48. Either/_____.
49. I will make of thee a _____ nation. (Gen. 12:2)
52. To be in poor health.
54. And it was _____. (Gen. 1:7)
56. Deed.
57. North Atlantic Treaty Organization (abbr.).
60. _____ thou not the oppressor. (Prov. 3:31)
61. As of fire, and it sat upon _____ of them. (Acts 2:3)
62. Thou shalt _____ eat of it. (Gen. 2:17)

DOWN CLUES

2. Plan.
3. Be ye lift up, ye _____ doors. (Ps.24:7)
4. Compass direction.
5. Rend.
6. And they shall be _____ flesh. (Gen. 2:24)
7. That in the _____ to come. (Eph. 2:7)
8. Total.
9. And the Lord God planted a _____. (Gen. 2:8)
10. Printer's measure.
13. Decree.
15. Both _____ and high. (Ps. 49:2)
18. Love _____ another. (John 15:17)
20. And I _____ eat. (Gen. 3:12)
22. There is none good but _____. (Matt. 19:17)
24. Child shall play on the hole of the _____. (Isa. 11:8)
25. The _____ beguiled me. (Gen. 3:13)
27. Pier.
30. Meadow.
33. _____ me, and know my thoughts. (Ps. 139:23)
34. Lefthanded judge. (Judg. 3:15)
35. Paddle.

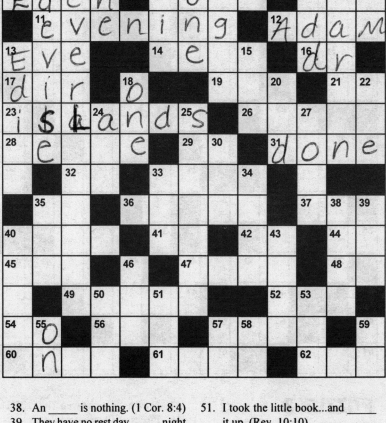

38. An _____ is nothing. (1 Cor. 8:4)
39. They have no rest day _____ night. (Rev. 14:11)
40. _____d is the ground for thy sake. (Gen. 3:17)
43. The _____ of the scornful. (Ps. 1:1)
46. Recreation (abbr.).
50. Beam.
51. I took the little book...and _____ it up. (Rev. 10:10)
53. Electrically charged atom.
55. Upon.
57. North Carolina (abbr.).
58. Exclamation.
59. _____ was very good. (Gen. 1:31)

PUZZLE 3

Helen Walter

ACROSS CLUES

1. Having _____ pieces of silver. (Luke 15:8)
4. I have found my sheep which was _____ (Luke 15:6)
7. Having a delicate open pattern.
11. A dried grape.
12. Enemy.
13. Vase.
14. I saw a _____ heaven. (Rev. 21:1)
16. Pieces of silver.
18. Direction.
19. Abraham set seven _____ lambs. (Gen. 21:28)
20. Entice.
21. Musical note.
23. Have a high regard for.
26. Signal for help.
28. _____ and outs.
29. That thou doest, _____ quickly. (John 13:27)
30. Woman's name.
31. Entreats earnestly.

33. Jacob's daughter. (Gen. 30:21)
35. _____ me, O Lord, in thy righ-
    teousness. (Ps. 5:8)
36. And they _____ out. (Mark 6:12)
37. He saw the spirit of God descend-
    ing like a _____. (Matt. 3:16)
39. Took possession.
42. Doctor.
46. Come _____ worship him.
    (Matt. 2:2)
47. Rock of _____.
48. California (abbr.).
49. _____ say, can you see?
51. Where _____ treasure is.
    (Matt. 6:21)
53. _____ a little while. (John 14:19)
54. Used for fishing.
55. Wandered.

DOWN CLUES

1. The judgments of the Lord are
   _____. (Ps. 19:9)
2. He that hath _____ to hear.
   (Mark 4:9)
3. Number of sheep safe in the fold.
   (Matt. 18:12)
4. Ending for fishing_____ or
   clothes_____.

5. In one direction only.
6. Toward.
8. Burning.
9. Ice cream _____.
10. Opposite of no.
15. Married.
16. Hold fast.
17. Us.
22. Individuality.
24. Stuck in the mud.
25. I am the _____ shepherd.
    (John 10:11)
26. Mother.
27. South American mountain range.
32. Like a grain of mustard _____.
    (Luke 13:19)
34. A garden tool.
38. I am Alpha and _____. (Rev. 1:8)
40. Animal home.
41. Arrow.
43. Frosted.
44. Domestic animal.
45. Thou art my beloved _____.
    (Luke 3:22)
50. _____ is not here. (Matt. 28:6)
52. Let _____ make man. (Gen. 1:26)
53. That _____ love one another.
    (John 13:34)

PUZZLE 4

Faith Wade

ACROSS CLUES

1. Filthy conversation of the _____. (2 Pet. 2:7)
4. Pekod, and Shoa, and _____. (Ezek. 23:23)
7. New Testament (abbr.).
9. His _____ is in the law. (Ps. 1:2)
11. _____ have we confidence toward God. (1 John 3:21)
15. Feline.
16. Be not, as the _____. (Matt. 6:16)
19. Hush.
20. When the wicked _____. (Prov. 11:10)
21. Let _____ many servants. (1 Tim. 6:1)
22. _____ not among thorns. (Jer. 4:3)
24. The son of _____, which was the son of Mattathias. (Luke 3:26)
26. Gaddiel the son of _____. (Num. 13:10)
27. Compass direction.
29. Bath-sheba's first husband. (2 Sam. 11:3)
30. Not down.
31. Negative.
32. Joshua sent men from Jericho to _____. (Josh. 7:2)
33. Mister (abbr.).
34. Newspaper want _____.
35. Rachel and Leah's father. (Gen. 29:10)
37. Lord, by thy _____. (Ps. 30:7)
39. By the hill of _____. (Judg. 7:1)
40. And ye are not your _____. (1 Cor. 6:19)
41. In _____ with God and men. (Luke 2:52; NAS)
43. Nathan... and Shimei, and _____. (1 Kgs. 1:8)
44. _____, and ye clothed me. (Matt. 25:36)
45. You and I.
46. Esau's color at birth. (Gen. 25:25)
47. Noah's boat.

DOWN CLUES

1. Every man _____ his weapons. (2 Chron. 23:7)
2. Short of Edwin.
3. They delivered them the _____. (Acts 16:4)
4. Javan, Elishah, and Tarshish, _____. (Gen. 10:4)
5. The kingdom of _____ in Bashan. (Deut. 3:4)
6. _____ was over the household. (1 Kgs. 4:6)
8. His dwelling among the _____. (Mark 5:3)
10. A lion's den.
12. Take a bunch of _____. (Ex. 12:22)
13. He made the _____ of gold. (Ex. 39:2)
14. Opposite of yes.
17. Computer Printer (abbr.).
18. Jacob's brother. (Gen. 25:2-26)
21. Benjamin's third child. (1 Chron. 8:1)
23. And there sat in a _____. (Acts 20:9)
25. Buy _____ and hewed stone. (2 Kgs. 12:12)
26. _____ the little children to come unto me. (Mark 10:14)
28. I am the _____. (John 15:6)
34. _____ it, pass not by it. (Prov. 4:15)
35. For God so _____. (John 3:16)
36. Of _____, the family of the Arodites. (Num. 26:17)

38. United Nations (abbr.).
39. Thou shall not _____ unto thee.
    (Ex. 20:4)
41. Not near.

42. _____, and it shall be given.
    (Matt. 7:7)
45. Abraham's hometown.
    (Gen. 11:31)

PUZZLE 5

Diana Rowland

ACROSS CLUES

1. He that earneth ____. (Hag. 1:6)
6. Let all ____ that seek thee rejoice. (Ps. 40:16)
11. Thou shalt ____. (Ps. 102:13)
12. Eliab the son of ____. (Num. 2:7)
13. And I will walk ____ liberty. (Ps. 119:45)
14. He hath settled on his ____, ____ hath not. (Jer. 48:11; 2 words)
16. The ungodly are not ____. (Ps. 1:4)
18. Exist.
19. Ark of God came to ____...for there was ____ deadly... (1 Sam. 5:10, 11; 2 words)
20. On the east side of ____. (Num. 34:11)
21. ____ also the Jairite was ____ chief ruler. (2 Sam. 20:26; 2 words)
23. How great is the ____ of them! (Ps. 139:17)
24. Thou hast also turned the ____. (Ps. 89:43)
25. As for such as turn ____ unto. (Ps. 125:5)
27. More than twelve ____ of angels? (Matt. 26:53)
29. Who is a ____ but he that denieth. (1 John 2:22)
31. Thou art ____ ____ God that.... (Ps. 5:4; 2 words)
32. ____ will ____ his hand also in ____ sea. (Ps. 89:25; 3 words)
35. ____, so would we...them ____ say. (Ps. 35:25; 2 words)
38. And ____ out of the valley. (Ps. 60:6)
39. Lyric poem.
41. Beyond the tower of ____. (Gen. 35:21)

42. National Institutes of Health (abbr.).
43. Transgressions as ____...multitude, ____ did.... (Job 31:33, 34; 2 words)
45. Texas Instruments (abbr.).
46. I have given ____ unto the children. (Deut. 2:9)
47. Borders of Archi to ____. (Josh. 16:2)
48. Hewlett Packard (abbr.).
49. Unto thy father that ____ thee. (Prov. 23:22)
51. They that sow in ____. (Ps. 126:5)
53. And ____ the lamp of God...down ____ sleep. (1 Sam. 3:3; 2 words)
54. To ____ thee good at thy latter ____. (Deut 8:16; 2 words, reverse order)

DOWN CLUES

1. Beside the still ____. (Ps. 23:2)
2. Given ____ unto the children. (Deut. 2:9)
3. Of Brazillai the ____. (Ezra 2:61)
4. He called the name of the well ____. (Gen. 26:20)
5. Then shall the ____ be ashamed. (Micah 3:7)
6. Obey God rather ____ ____. (Acts 5:29; 2 words)
7. City of Sepharvaim, ____, and Ivah? (Is. 37:13)
8. God is my King of ____. (Ps. 74:12)
9. I am ____ troubled. (Ps. 77:4)
10. Lifted up as an ____ upon his land. (Zech. 9:16)
13. Of the course of ____. (Luke 1:5)
15. He restoreth my ____. (Ps. 23:3)
17. May fall by his strong ____. (Ps. 10:10)
20. Why make ye this ____, ____ weep? (Mark 5:39; 2 words)

22. What _____ thee now. (Is. 22:1)
24. And _____ taken...not any, _____ great. (1 Sam. 30:2; 2 words, reverse order)
26. The meek shall _____. (Ps. 22:26)
28. Called to _____ out into _____ place. (Heb. 11:8; 2 words)
30. A damsel came _____ hearken, named _____. (Acts 12:13; 2 words, reverse order)
32. Zophah, and _____, and Shelesh. (1 Chron. 7:35)
33. _____ also shall _____ a possession. (Num. 24:18; 2 words)

34. Beyond the tower of _____. (Gen. 35:21)
36. Quit of thine _____...words, _____ be it. (Josh. 2:20,21; 2 words)
37. Voyage, flight, or drive.
40. To speak in a theatrical manner.
43. Discovered _____ thy rebuke, O Lord, _____. (Ps. 18:15; 2 words)
44. _____ God:...of _____ strings. (Ps. 144:9; 2 words)
47. Mine _____ is as nothing. (Ps. 39:5)
50. The sons of Judah were _____. (Num. 26:19)
52. Rural Delivery (abbr.).

13

PUZZLE 6

Teresa Zeek

ACROSS CLUES

1. He was hidden in the bulrushes. (Ex. 2:3, 10)
5. Another name for Saul. (Acts 13:9)
8. _____ ye into all the world. (Mark 16:15)
10. There was no room in the _____. (Luke 2:7)
11. To rule _____ the day and ... night (Gen. 1:18)
13. _____. Even so, come, Lord Jesus. (Rev. 22:20)
15. Flashing _____ lights.
17. He _____ there an altar. (Gen. 33:20)
19. Stops nursing.
20. Masculine pronoun.
21. Suffix used to make a comparative word.
24. A very small quantity.
26. Prefix meaning "three."
27. Female deer.
29. The wicked have laid a _____ for me. (Ps. 119:110)
32. A set of three.
34. To be carried.
36. Scrooge says, "_____ humbug."
38. Minnesota (abbr.).
39. It was planted in a good _____. (Ezek. 17:8)
40. A swarm of _____. (Judg. 14:8)
41. Churning of milk bringeth forth _____. (Prov. 30:33)
43. Dominion over the fowl of the _____. (Gen. 1:26)
44. Support or brace.
46. Wipe your feet on our welcome _____.

48. Whoso keepeth the commandment shall _____ no evil thing. (Ec. 8:5)
49. Demonstration model (abbr.).
50. King of Moab. (Judg. 3:17)
53. Yellow tropical fruit.
56. God created the heaven and the _____. (Gen. 1:1)
57. Mary stayed with Elisabeth three _____. (Luke 1:56)

DOWN CLUES

1. Love the Lord with all thy heart,... soul, and..._____. (Matt. 22:37)
2. The Lord our God is _____ Lord. (Deut. 6:4)
3. Sins...as white as _____. (Isa. 1:18)
4. Even _____, come Lord Jesus. (Rev. 22:20)
5. The express image of his _____. (Heb. 1:3)
6. Blessed _____ the poor in spirit. (Matt. 5:3)
7. It is vain...to sit up _____. (Ps. 127:2)
8. The king of Debir, one; the king of _____. (Josh. 12:13)
9. Putting _____ the breastplate of faith and love. (1 Thes. 5:8)
12. Take me some _____. (Gen. 27:3)
14. "Jesus loves _____, this I know."
16. I will _____ leave thee. (Heb. 13:5)
18. Some trust in _____, and some in horses. (Ps. 20:7)
22. Christ has _____.
23. Advertisement (abbr.).
25. Saul of _____. (Acts 9:11)
28. Charity...toward each _____ aboundeth. (2 Thes. 1:3)
30. To revise.
31. _____, Father, all things are possible unto thee. (Mark 14:36)
33. I am (contraction).

35. The _____s shall melt with fervent heat. (2 Pet. 3:10)
37. The first three vowels.
41. Light_____.
42. Elkanah's home. (1 Sam. 2:11)
44. They went into one _____. (2 Kgs. 7:8)
45. Second tone of the diatonic scale.
47. Its waves thereof _____ themselves. (Jer. 5:22)
48. _____ God so loved the world. (John 3:16)
49. Rachel's maid, Bilhah's first son. (Gen. 30:56)
51. General Electric (abbr.).
52. Sixth tone of the diatonic scale.
54. I _____ THAT I AM. (Ex. 3:14)
55. Let _____ man deceive you. (2 Thes. 2:3)

PUZZLE 7

Janice Buhl

ACROSS CLUES

1. Are thou the _____ of the Jews? (Luke 23:3)
4. I am not _____ to destroy. (Matt. 5:17)
7. Do, re, me, _____.
9. _____ said unto Samuel, Go, lie down. (1 Sam. 3:9)
10. Abihail the son of _____. (1 Chron. 5:14)
11. Tuberculosis (abbr.).
13. She gave me of the tree, and I did _____. (Gen. 3:12)
14. Gold, silver, ivory, and _____ and peacocks. (1 Kgs. 10:22)
15. Full ears of corn in the _____ thereof. (2 Kgs. 4:42)
17. _____ king of Jarmuth. (Josh. 10:3)
19. Poured out my soul _____ the Lord. (1 Sam. 1:15)
21. The sons of Judah were _____ and Onan. (Num. 26:19)
23. The glory of the Lord shone _____ about them. (Luke 2:9)
24. Saint (abbr.).
26. Be as an _____ whose leaf fadeth. (Isa. 1:30)
27. Go _____ therefore. (Matt. 28:19)
28. _____ we love one another. (1 John 4:12)
29. Cut off his thumbs and his great _____. (Judg. 1:6)
31. And _____ came to pass. (Judg. 1:14)
33. Before the judgment of _____ of Christ. (Rom. 14:10)
36. Part in a play.
37. Take thou unto thee an iron _____. (Ezek. 4:3)
38. Your labour is not in _____. (1 Cor. 15:58)
39. It shall go _____ with him that is left. (Job 20:26)
40. Nothing.
41. Cain talked with _____ his brother. (Gen. 4:8)
43. _____ with joy receiveth it. (Matt. 13:20)
44. The _____, which they saw in the east. (Matt. 2:9)
47. Lo, the wicked _____ their bow. (Ps. 11:2)
49. Go to the _____, thou sluggard. (Prov. 6:6)
50. The beginning and the _____. (Rev. 22:13)
51. Noble poem.
52. So many _____ of voices. (1 Cor. 14:10)

DOWN CLUES

1. The Lord bless thee and _____ thee. (Num. 6:24)
2. _____ the Ahohite. (1 Chron. 11:29)
3. Wash thee with _____. (Jer. 2:22)
4. Ye cannot drink the _____ of the Lord. (1 Cor. 10:21)
5. They slew _____ upon the rock. (Judg. 7:25)
6. Thou shalt forget thy _____. (Job 11:16)
8. _____, and it shall be given you. (Luke 11:9)
10. Shem, _____, and Japheth. (Gen. 5:32)
11. _____ shalt deny me thrice. (Mark 14:30)
12. Did not our heart _____ within us? (Luke 24:32)

16

16. Him that for _____ and murder was cast into prison. (Luke 23:25)
18. Deborah _____, and went with Barak. (Judg. 4:9)
20. Until I make thy _____ thy foot stool. (Acts 2:35)
22. To _____ like a calf. (Ps. 29:6)
24. Long, narrow pieces.
25. Not lift up any iron _____ upon them. (Deut. 27:5)
30. Building wing.
32. Preparest a _____ before me (Ps. 23:5)

34. We have one father, _____ God. (John 8:41)
35. Is not _____ the Levite thy brother? (Ex. 4:14)
40. _____ the son of Ahitub. (2 Sam. 8:17)
41. Who _____ thou, Lord? (Acts 9:5)
42. Gaal the son of _____. (Judg. 9:26)
45. Convert skins to leather.
46. _____ it shall come to pass. (Ex. 4:9)
48. And the earth _____ without form. (Gen. 1:2)

PUZZLE 8

Janet Adkins

ACROSS CLUES

1. A sword is upon the liars; and they shall _____. (Jer. 50:36)
4. A little oil in a _____. (1 Kgs. 17:12)
8. The glory which thou gavest _____. (John 17:22)
10. Bringing gold, silver, ivory, and _____(s). (1 Kgs. 10:22)
11. I will _____ out my spirit unto you. (Prov. 1:23)
12. Calf meat.
14. Thou...hast _____ forth the people. (Ex. 15:13)
15. Sounds of hesitation.
16. Whose names are in the _____ of life. (Phil. 4:3)
17. They could not enter _____ because of unbelief. (Heb. 3:19)
18. True _____, help those women which laboured. (Phil. 4:3)
20. Even as a _____ gathereth her chickens. (Matt. 23:37; plural)
21. Roman numeral 6.
23. Like
24. Egyptian god.
26. Doth not _____ one of you on the sabbath loose his ox? (Luke 13:15)
28. One who installs or endows.
31. See thou tell _____ man. (Matt. 8:4)
32. As he thinketh in his heart _____ is _____. (Prov. 23:7; 2 words)
33. Grain.
35. Border state (abbr.).
37. Do all things without _____urings. (Phil. 2:14)
38. Short for Elizabeth.
40. Erie law enforcement agency.
41. Made you _____s to feed the church. (Acts 20:28, archaic)
43. They shall build houses and _____ it them. (Isa. 65:21)
45. Orderly.
46. Southwestern state (abbr.).
47. Yesterday (Spanish).
49. Route (abbr.).
50. Greek letter.
51. Ye shall be unto _____ a kingdom of priests. (Ex. 19:6)
52. And the king was _____. (Matt. 14:9)
53. The _____ head fell into the water. (2 Kgs. 6:5, alt. spelling)

DOWN CLUES

1. Surrealist artist.
2. Ye shall see heaven _____. (John 1:51)
3. Senator _____ Kennedy.
4. Wine bottle stoppers.
5. A type of trick.
6. Went forth with them from _____ of the Chaldees. (Gen. 11:31)
7. Man was created, did not _____.
8. Dangerous shark.
9. "Strength" (Heb.).
11. Unskillled worker.
13. Carried by the wind.
16. Let him _____ Anathema Marantha. (1 Cor. 16:22)
18. A thousand years in thy sight are but as _____. (Ps. 90:4; plural)
19. Yah_____.
20. Children of Ziha, the children of _____. (Neh. 7:46)
22. Publican...would not lift up so much as _____ eyes. (Luke 18:13)
24. Let us _____ together. (Isa. 1:18)

25. Thou _____ the man. (2 Sam. 12:7)
27. In whatsoever state I am, therewith to be _____. (Phil. 4:11)
29. System of naming things: _____clature.
30. I go unto Jerusalem _____ minister unto the saints. (Rom. 15:25)
34. Covet earnestly the _____ gifts. (1 Cor. 12:31)
36. Pertaining to the skin.
38. Rude child.
39. Symbol for tellurium.
42. Weird. (alt. spelling)
43. Belief system (suffix).
44. Mixed-up Elks Club.
48. Northern Pacific or B&O _____. (abbr.).
50. Former mate.

19

PUZZLE 9

Rebecca Souder

ACROSS CLUES

1. The patience of _____. (Jam. 5:11)
4. Messenger of God.
8. _____ so loved the world. (John 3:16)
10. Before.
11. There was _____ room for them. (Luke 2:7)
12. _____ be taxed with Mary. (Luke 2:5)
13. To place.
14. Mary's hometown. (Luke 1:26)
18. Exclamation of triumph.
19. The angel appeared to Joseph in a _____. (Matt. 1:20)
20. Son of Noah. (Gen. 6:10)
23. Valley where David fought Goliath. (1 Sam. 17:2)
25. Noah's second son.
28. Licenses Surgeon (abbr.).
31. Elizabeth (variation).
34. Pale.
37. About.
38. True.
40. Buzzing insect.
41. His _____ drew the third part of the stars. (Rev. 12:4)
43. Therefore, I _____ you. (Rom. 12:1 NIV)
44. Burnt offerings of _____. (Isa. 1:11)
45. District Attorney (abbr.).
46. Time in office.
47. And _____ came to pass. (Luke 1:41)
48. Mary's husband. (Matt. 1:20)
51. Life story (abbr.).
53. Rear Admiral (abbr.).

54. New (prefix).
56. _____, the angel of the Lord. (Luke 2:9)
57. Cyrenius was his governor. (Luke 2:2)
58. _____, and it shall be given. (Matt. 7:7)

DOWN CLUES

1. The Son of God.
2. Mine product.
3. He called the name of that place _____. (Gen. 28:19)
4. A prophetess. (Luke 2:36)
5. He built an ark.
6. Greek vowel.
7. The angel of the _____.
8. Entrance.
9. _____ to others. (Matt. 7:12 NIV)
15. Father of John. (Luke 1:59)
16. Make a mistake.
17. _____, thou that are highly favoured. (Luke 1:28)
21. _____ shall be called John. (Luke 1:60)
22. Every _____ that openeth the womb. (Luke 2:23)
24. Clue.
26. Cain's brother.
27. Come unto _____. (Matt. 11:28)
29. Melchizedek king of _____. (Gen. 14:18)
30. The angel _____. (Luke 1:26)
32. I am the way, the _____, and the life. (John 14:6)
33. It is good for us to be _____. (Matt. 17:4)
35. They sit in Moses' _____. (Matt. 23:2)
36. Touched the _____ of his garment. (Matt. 9:20)

20

39. Concurs.
42. Fuss.
48. Good tidings of great _____.
    (Luke 2:10)
49. Historic period.

50. Cooking pot.
52. Unto you _____ born this day.
    (Luke 2:11)
54. Not Available (abbr.).
55. All right.

PUZZLE 10

Rebecca Souder

ACROSS CLUES

1. With him on the sacred _____.
   (2 Pet. 1:18 NIV)
6. And to brotherly kindness, _____.
   (2 Pet. 1:7 NIV).
9. Absent (abbr.).
10. Division of Scripture.
11. _____, I am with you always.
    (Matt. 28:20)
12. Biblical beast used in the fields.
13. Our Savior _____ Christ.
16. Combining form meaning "having fruit."
18. Hebrew combining form for "God."
19. Thy word is a _____ unto my feet.
    (Ps. 119:105)
22. Draw out.
23. A more _____ word of prophecy.
    (2 Pet. 1:19)
25. Spoken.
26. Religion (abbr.).
27. Half of a kind of fly.
28. Not amateur.
29. A movie rating.
30. No prophecy of the _____ is of any private interpretation. (2 Pet. 1:20)
34. Jacob's first wife.
35. Pea's home.
36. Noah...a _____ of righteousness.
    (2 Pet. 2:5)
38. Lieutenant (abbr.).
39. _____ else.
40. Our Lord Jesus _____.
43. Received from God...honour and _____. (2 Pet. 1:17)
44. They are all gone _____. (Ps. 14:3)
46. Self.
48. Food regimen.
49. Thy _____ and thy staff. (Ps. 23:4)
50. From his old _____. (2 Pet. 1:9)
51. When _____ made known unto you.
    (2 Pet. 1:16)

DOWN CLUES

1. Were eyewitnesses of his _____.
   (2 Pet. 1:16)
2. A mark used in old manuscripts.
3. United States Ship (abbr.).
4. Indefinite article.
5. He, she, and _____.
6. Our _____ Jesus Christ.
7. There came such a _____ to him.
   (2 Pet. 1:17)
8. From the _____ glory. (2 Pet. 1:17)
11. The father of Eliasaph. (Num. 3:24)
14. Suffix meaning "small."
15. South America (abbr.).
17. Cleaned totally.
20. Land where Abraham offered Isaac. (Gen. 22:2)
21. For the _____ came not...by the will of man. (2 Pet. 1:21)
24. Reserve (abbr.).
28. Great and _____ promises.
    (2 Pet. 1:4)
29. Through faith...obtained _____.
    (Heb. 11:33)
31. Quahog is another word for a _____ m.
32. Direction.
33. If any of you do _____ from the truth. (Jam. 5:19)
36. The _____ and coming of our Lord.
    (2 Pet. 1:16)
37. Blood factor.
38. Company (British abbr.).
41. He prayed...that it might not _____.
    (Jam. 5:17)

42. Make all _____. (Mark 6:39)
43. Holy men of _____ spake. (2 Pet. 1:21)
45. Were _____ witnesses. (2 Pet. 1:16)

47. _____ ye unto all the world. (Mark 16:15)
48. Roman numeral 501.

PUZZLE 11

Karen Kapferer

ACROSS CLUES

1. Behold, I shew you a _____.
   (1 Cor. 15:51)
6. He blessed Samuel. (1 Sam. 1:25)
8. Roe or hart.
9. Las Vegas (abbr.).
10. Tohu was the son of _____.
    (1 Sam. 1:1)
12. _____ killed his brother, Abel.
    (Gen. 4:8)
14. Negative.
15. Major airline (abbr.).
18. _____ out my transgressions.
    (Ps. 51:1)
19. A gift brought to Jesus. (Matt. 2:11)
21. City in Norway.
22. Someone looked up to or admired.
23. Royal Ambassador (abbr.).
24. _____omans, _____saiah,
    _____amentations.
26. Either/_____.
27. The _____ in heart shall be filled
    with his own ways. (Prov. 14:14)
32. He, _____, it.
33. City in Alaska.
34. Daniel, Isaiah, Amos, etc.
37. Who...had seen the grace of God,
    was _____. (Acts 11:23)
38. Before Abraham was, _____ _____.
    (John 8:58; 2 words)
39. Omri's son who became king.
    (1 Kgs. 16:29)
41. Win, lose, _____.
42. Ocean Pacific (abbr.).
43. Receive not the grace of God in
    _____. (2 Cor. 6:1)

46. This animal rebuked Balaam.
    (Num. 22:28)
47. To return to an earlier state.
48. Company (abbr.)
49. The _____ killeth, but the spirit
    giveth life. (2 Cor. 3:6)
50. The _____ shall rejoice. (Isa. 35:1)

DOWN CLUES

2. Ye _____, submit yourselves unto
   the elder. (1 Pet. 5:5)
3. Edward (abbr.).
4. The vail of the temple was _____.
   (Matt. 27:51)
5. You (biblical).
6. Speak _____ of no man. (Titus 3:2)
7. Not out.
9. The sleep of a _____ man is sweet.
   (Ec. 5:12; Am. spelling)
11. For your sakes he became _____.
    (2 Cor. 8:9)
13. Jesus healed the son of a _____.
    (John 4:46-50)
16. Tribulation _____ patience.
    (Rom. 5:3)
17. Whose mother was removed from
    being queen? (1 Kgs. 15:9-13)
20. A slow-moving tennis ball.
22. Institution for the sick.
25. Graven image.
28. Tree mentioned in Isaiah 44:14.
29. Less expensive.
30. A primary color.
31. Remember me when thou _____
    into thy kingdom. (Luke 23:42)
35. He...shall _____ up us also.
    (2 Cor. 4:14)
36. Thy faith hath _____ thee.
    (Luke 7:50)

40. Thou sowest...but _____ grain. (1 Cor. 15:37)
42. Iron.
44. It is.
45. I _____ that through ignorance ye did it. (Acts 3:17)
48. Credit (abbr.).

PUZZLE 12

Diana Rowland

ACROSS CLUES

1. _____ him in a manager. (Luke 2:7)
5. _____, the beloved physician. (Col. 4:14)
9. Standing afar _____...to me _____ sinner. (Luke 18:13; 2 words)
10. The name of the well _____. (Gen. 26:20)
11. And sold a _____ for wine. (Joel 3:3)
13. Will _____ rather say unto him. (Luke 17:8)
15. Beautician's wave.
18. The elder unto the elect _____. (2 John 1)
19. I _____ me men singers. (Ec. 2:8)
20. For every _____ is known by his own fruit. (Luke 6:44)
21. They marvelled _____ his answer. (Luke 20:26)
22. Come down _____ my child die. (John 4:49)
23. Many shall rejoice _____ his birth. (Luke 1:14)
24. I am _____ both to the Greeks. (Rom. 1:14)
28. _____ ye from him. (2 Sam. 11:15)
32. On the east side of _____. (Num. 34:11)
33. _____ the father of Abner. (1 Sam. 14:51)
34. Shelemiah the son of _____. (Jer. 36:26)
37. _____ the son of Jeroham. (1 Chron. 9:12)
40. So shall it _____ also in the days. (Luke 17:26)
41. His mother's name also was _____. (2 Kgs. 18:2)
43. _____ is not here, but is risen. (Luke 24:6)

44. Eloi, _____ lama sabachthani? (Mark 15:34)
47. _____, I say unto you. (Luke 7:26)
48. And Hushim, the sons of _____. (1 Chron. 7:12)
50. Behold the _____ of God. (John 1:29)
51. Love worketh no _____ to his neighbour. (Rom. 13:10)
52. The wicked _____ their bow. (Ps. 11:2)
53. Of _____, the family of the Eranites. (Num. 26:36)
55. Kish the son of _____. (2 Chron. 29:12)
57. Put a _____ on his hand. (Luke 15:22)
58. Every _____ at the feast of the passover. (Luke 2:41)

DOWN CLUES

1. Lo, the angel of the _____ came upon them. (Luke 2:9)
2. Of _____ great eagle, that she might _____. (Rev. 12:14; 2 words)
3. _____ thou be the Son of God. (Luke 4:3)
4. Is in _____ of eternal damnation. (Mark 3:29)
5. He wrote a _____ after this manner. (Acts 23:25)
6. He followeth not with _____. (Luke 9:49)
7. All these have I _____ from my youth up. (Luke 18:21)
8. Jamin, and _____. (1 Chron. 2:27)
11. He was exceeding _____. (Luke 23:8)
12. _____ _____ no pleasant bread. (Dan. 10:3; 2 words)
14. All that handle the _____. (Ezek. 27:29)
16. Wilt thou _____ it up in three days? (John 2:20)
17. That ye _____ withal it shall be. (Luke 6:38)

26

25. Cast the _____ away. (Matt. 13:48)
26. _____ them about thy neck. (Prov. 6:21)
27. But _____ thing is needful. (Luke 10:42)
29. Of his kingdom there shall be no _____. (Luke 1:33)
30. Hot beverage.
31. Jerimoth, and _____, five. (1 Chron. 7:7)
34. From the blood of _____ unto the blood. (Luke 11:51)
35. When _____ was dead. (1 Chron. 1:44)
36. _____ wait for him. (Luke 11:54)
37. Do to _____ and her king...shall ye take for _____ prey..._____ thee an ambush. (Josh. 8:2; 3 words)
38. Even as _____ _____ gathereth her chickens. (Matt. 23:37; 2 words)
39. There was there an _____ of many swine. (Luke 8:32)
42. I will punish _____ in Babylon. (Jer. 51:44)
45. Fill an _____ of it to be kept. (Ex. 16:32)
46. Zaccur, and _____. (1 Chron. 24:27)
48. The son of _____ was over the tribute. (1 Kgs. 4:6)
49. This is the _____. (Luke 20:14)
54. They might find _____ accusation. (Luke 6:7)
56. All shall _____ thine. (Luke 4:7)

27

PUZZLE 13

Evelyn M. Boyington

ACROSS CLUES

1. But _____ unto you. (Matt. 23:13)
4. A time to rend, and a time to _____. (Ec. 3:7)
7. The name of his city was _____. (1 Chron. 1:50)
10. The children of Aram; Uz, and _____. (Gen. 10:23)
11. Upon the great _____ of their right foot. (Ex. 29:20)
12. God...is _____ to deliver us. (Dan. 3:17)
14. Source.
16. You fathers, where _____ they? (Zech. 1:5)
17. _____ no violence to the stranger. (Jer. 22:3)
19. Eye hath not seen, nor _____ heard. (1 Cor. 2:9)
20. Fear and the _____, and the snare, are upon thee. (Isa. 24:17)
21. Ye have made it a _____ of thieves. (Mark 11:17)
22. Thou didst _____ on the Lord. (2 Chron. 16:8)
24. Golf score.
25. She bound the scarlet _____ in the window. (Josh. 2:21)
26. 4 in Roman numerals.
27. All they are brass, and _____, and iron. (Ezek. 22:18)
28. He _____ to meet him. (Gen. 29:13)
29. Joseph was a goodly _____. (Gen. 39:6)
32. _____ me, and be merciful unto me. (Ps. 26:11)
35. Edible grain.
36. Pronoun.
37. Why are _____ so fearful? (Mark 4:40)
38. My yoke is _____. (Matt. 11:30)
40. His eyes shall be _____ with wine. (Gen. 49:12)
41. Promises of God in him are yea, and in him _____. (2 Cor. 1:20)

43. How long will it be _____ thou be quiet? (Jer. 47:6)
44. _____ also, which went with Abram. (Gen. 13:5)
45. He maketh me to _____ down in green pastures. (Ps. 23:2)
46. Southern state (abbr.).
47. Their _____ calveth. (Job 21:10)
48. _____ smoke the ass. (Num. 22:23)
51. Early day.
53. Were there not _____ cleansed? (Luke 17:17)
54. Article.
55. Cereal grain.
56. The _____ number of them. (Num. 3:48)
57. Make us _____ together in heavenly places. (Eph. 2:6)

DOWN CLUES

1. _____ hath believed our report. (Isa. 53:1)
2. _____ Father which art in heaven. (Matt. 6:9)
3. _____ the Mahavite. (1 Chron. 11:46)
4. _____ up the gift of God. (2 Tim. 1:6)
5. Age.
6. When _____ were children. (Gal. 4:3)
7. The Lord taketh my _____ with them that help me. (Ps. 118:7)
8. Lincoln.
9. 49 in Roman numerals.
13. God planted a garden eastward in _____. (Gen. 2:8)
15. Respect to him that weareth the _____ clothing. (Jam. 2:3)
16. The birds of the _____ have nests. (Matt. 8:20)
18. Not _____ thing hath failed. (Josh. 23:14)
20. She took a _____, and poured them out. (2 Sam. 13:9)
21. Come and _____. (John 21:12)
22. Tear.
23. Adam called his wife's name _____. (Gen. 3:20)

24. She fastened it with the _____. (Judg. 16:14)
25. There is a _____ here. (John 6:9)
27. Young child.
28. Peleg... begat _____. (Gen. 11:18)
30. I am the _____ of Sharon. (Song of Sol. 2:1)
31. Consider what I _____. (2 Tim. 2:7)
32. Thy _____ and thy staff they comfort me. (Ps. 23:4)
33. _____ hath not seen. (1 Cor. 2:9)
34. It is appointed unto _____ once to die. (Heb. 9:27)
36. It doth not _____ appear what we shall be. (1 John 3:2)
38. Lamprey.
39. Balak... hath brought me from _____. (Num. 23:7)

40. Put pure frankincense upon each _____. (Lev. 24:7)
41. To be troubled.
42. Neither desire thou his dainty _____. (Prov. 23:6)
44. Solitary.
45. Let the dry _____ appear. (Gen. 1:9)
47. Unto thee will I _____, O Lord. (Ps. 28:1)
48. David arose from off his _____. (2 Sam. 11:2)
49. _____ the son of Abdiel. (1 Chron. 5:15)
50. The angels of God _____ him. (Gen. 32:1)
52. Conjunction.
53. It is not for you _____ know. (Acts 1:7)

29

PUZZLE 14

Evelyn M. Boyington

ACROSS CLUES

1. Enemy.
4. _____ shalt thou serve. (Deut. 10:20)
7. Beno, and Shoham, and Zaccur, and _____. (1 Chron. 24:27)
11. All the rivers _____ into the sea. (Ec. 1:7)
12. Provoked the _____ One of Israel unto anger. (Is. 1:4)
13. The city had no _____ of the sun. (Rev. 21:23)
14. One who decrees.
16. Urn.
17. The Pharisees began to _____ him vehemently. (Luke 11:53)
18. Happenings.
20. Thou shalt not call her name Sarai, but _____. (Gen. 17:15)
22. Every one beareth _____s. (Song of Sol. 6:6)
23. Anab, and Eshtemoh, and _____. (Josh. 15:50)
24. The slothful man _____ not that which he took in hunting. (Prov. 12:27)
28. Unit of weight.
29. A distinct type.
30. Born.
31. Etched.
33. The bright and morning _____. (Rev. 22:16)
34. To whom be glory for _____. (Rom. 11:36)
35. Thou art _____. (Ps. 139:8)
36. Thou shalt not make unto thee any _____ image. (Ex. 20:4)
39. The fathers have eaten a _____ grape. (Jer. 31:29)
40. The desert shall rejoice, and blossom as the _____. (Is. 35:1)
41. The biology of heredity.
45. A thought.
46. Ages.
47. Until the day that _____ entered into the ark. (Luke 17:27)
48. Then bring _____. And he cast it into the pot. (2 Kgs. 4:41)
49. Till I shall _____ about it. (Luke 13:8)
50. Acquired.

DOWN CLUES

1. We have walked to and_____ through the earth. (Zech. 1:11)
2. _____ Father which art in heaven. (Matt. 6:9)
3. Ye have in heaven a better and an _____ substance. (Heb. 10:34)
4. Sharpening stone.
5. French island.
6. I come quickly; and _____ _____ is with me. (Rev. 22:12; 2 words)
7. _____ to themselves instruments of musick. (Amos 6:5)
8. Lima or snap.
9. They _____ not day and night. (Rev. 4:8)
10. March date.
12. For the Lord most _____ is terrible. (Ps. 47:2)
15. Esrom begat _____. (Matt. 1:3)
19. Clamp.
20. Satisfy.
21. And _____ they tell him of her. (Mark 1:30)
24. Hath greatly offended, and _____ himself upon them. (Ezek. 25:12)

25. And _____ into the sepulchre, they saw a young man. (Mark 16:5)
26. _____ their claws in pieces. (Zech. 11:16)
27. Behold, _____ I am. (1 Sam. 12:3)
29. Wherefore God also _____ them up to uncleanness. (Rom. 1:24)
32. He to whom the Son will _____ him. (Luke 10:22)
33. The Lord _____ him in. (Gen. 7:16)
35. Thou sawest the feet and _____. (Dan. 2:41)
36. Forbidding.
37. Jehu _____ in a chariot. (2 Kgs. 9:16)
38. Am I ___ _____, or a whale? (Job 7:12; 2 words)
39. Catch.
42. Airport code to Erie, Pennsylvania.
43. Pigeon sound.
44. _____ thine house in order. (Isa. 38:1)

31

PUZZLE 15

Valerie Barrett

ACROSS CLUES

1. Joseph's firstborn. (Gen. 41:51)
10. Kings of armies did flee _____. (Ps. 68:12)
11. Then _____ my present. (Gen. 33:10)
14. _____ with her suburbs. (Josh. 21:32)
16. Cut off the ropes of the _____. (Acts 27:32)
17. Do they not _____ that device evil? (Prov. 14:22)
18. Gather a certain _____ every day. (Ex. 16:4)
20. Greatly _____ be praised. (Ps. 48:1)
21. Built there an altar, and called the place _____ beth-el. (Gen. 35:7)
22. Had devils long time, and _____ no clothes. (Luke 8:27)
25. Noah begat three sons, _____, Ham, and Japheth. (Gen. 6:10)
26. Puttest thy _____ in a rock. (Num. 24:21)
27. _____, every one that thirsteth. (Is. 55:1)
28. Judge me, O God, _____ plead. (Ps. 43:1)
31. Shechem which is in the land of _____. (Gen. 33:18)
33. For the _____ that is in the land of Assyria. (Isa. 7:18)
34. Ye shall not _____ my face. (Gen. 43:3)
36. They _____ to and fro. (Ps. 107:27; past tense)
38. Thou art Simon the son of _____. (John 1:42)

40. Driven up and down in _____. (Acts 27:27)
42. As the _____, because he cheweth the cud. (Lev. 11:4)
44. Benjamin's _____ was five times. (Gen. 43:34)
45. Men shall _____ him out of his place. (Job 27:23)
46. _____ was concubine to Eliphaz. (Gen. 36:12)

DOWN CLUES

1. I will _____ thy seed to multiply. (Gen. 26:4)
2. Thou shalt set _____ unto the Lord. (Ex. 13:12)
3. There were _____ windows. (Ezek. 41:26)
4. To pass his _____, his strange act. (Isa. 28:21)
5. Israel went into the midst of the _____. (Ex. 14:22)
6. _____, Judah's firstborn. (Gen. 38:7)
7. Two men of the _____s strove. (Ex. 2:13)
8. An adder...that _____ the horse. (Gen. 49:17)
9. They shall _____ ashamed. (Hosea 4:19)
12. Having a live _____ in his hand. (Isa. 6:6)
13. Thou shalt not _____ of it. (Gen. 2:17)
15. The _____ of the children of Israel. (Ex. 28:9)
19. They shall call his name _____. (Matt. 1:23)
23. _____ unjust man is an abomination. (Prov. 29:27)

24. Cast them into the _____ _____. (Ex. 10:19)
25. And thou his _____, O Belshazzar. (Dan. 5:22)
27. Sons of Reuben: _____, and Phallu. (Gen. 46:9)
28. So _____ departed, as the Lord had spoken. (Gen. 12:4)
29. As though he _____ any thing. (Acts 17:25)
30. The roebuck, and the fallow _____(s). (Deut. 14:5)
32. The similitude of _____ transgression. (Rom. 5:14)
35. The children of Gad called the altar _____. (Josh. 22:34)
37. Whithersoever the governor _____eth. (Jam. 3:4)
39. Heber's wife took a _____ of the tent. (Judg. 4:21)
41. Cast down your slain _____. (Ezek. 6:4)
43. The abbreviation for the 17th book of the Old Testament.

PUZZLE 16

Valerie Barrett

ACROSS CLUES

1. The _____ said unto the younger. (Gen. 19:31)
7. The kingdom of _____ king of Bashan. (Num. 32:33)
9. He had _____ in the grave four days. (John 11:17)
10. A greeting.
11. Hear I _____ you, ye sons of Levi. (Num. 16:8)
13. A faithful _____ is health. (Prov. 13:17)
15. Nothing: _____ro.
16. Lord shall _____ to me another son. (Gen. 30:24)
17. _____ the son of Nathan. (2 Sam. 23:36)
18. With the _____ of the sword. (Gen. 34:26)
20. Bored a hole in the _____. (2 Kgs. 12:9)
21. Even _____ the tongue is a little member. (Jam. 3:5)
22. _____, the beloved physician. (Col. 4:14)
23. For, _____, the wicked bend their bow. (Ps. 11:2)
25. Blessed are ye that _____ beside all waters. (Isa. 32:20)
26. Achar, the troubler of _____. (1 Chron. 2:7)
30. Went forth to _____ into the land. (Gen. 12:5)
31. _____ that time the Lord said. (Deut. 10:1)
32. _____ the son of Kish. (1 Sam. 10:21)
34. Speak anything _____. (Dan. 3:29)
35. And _____ her brother said unto her. (2 Sam. 13:20)
40. The dove found _____ rest. (Gen. 8:9)
41. Filled with the _____ of the ointment. (John 12:3)
42. And if thy oblation _____ a meat offering. (Lev. 2:5)
43. _____ sinful nation. (Isa. 1:4)
45. Brought them unto _____ to see. (Gen. 2:19)
46. Which perished at _____dor. (Ps. 83:10)
47. An abbreviation for the third book before the New Testament; also an old, ugly woman.
48. _____ it in their hearts. (Jer. 31:33)
49. Offerings of the Lord made _____ fire. (Lev. 24:9)

DOWN CLUES

1. Their faces shall be as _____. (Isa. 13:8)
2. God said unto Moses. _____ _____. (Ex. 3:14)
3. They smote him under the fifth _____. (2 Sam. 4:6)
4. Shall this man be a _____ unto us. (Ex. 10:7)
5. Jemuel, and Jamin, and _____. (Gen. 46:10)
6. I will now put forth a _____ unto you. (Judg. 14:12)
7. Whether poor _____ rich. (Ruth 3:10)
8. Baldness is come upon _____. (Jer. 47:5)
11. I will break the _____ of your power. (Lev. 26:19)
12. Feathers with _____ gold. (Ps. 68:13)

14. But _____ ministered before the Lord. (1 Sam. 2:18)

19. In his word _____ I hope. (Ps. 130:5)

23. One _____ for the Lord. (Lev. 16:8)

24. This great fire will _____ us. (Deut. 5:25)

25. As he was about to _____ into Syria. (Acts 20:3)

26. The vision of _____ the son of Amoz. (Isa. 1:1)

27. A shortened name for the ninth book of the Old Testament.

28. Let this _____ be under thy hand. (Isa. 3:6)

29. The Lord _____ will be a refuge. (Ps. 9:9)

33. Of Manasseh, _____ the son of Susi. (Num. 13:11)

36. And there went over a ferry _____. (2 Sam. 19:18)

37. It hath consumed _____ of Moab. (Num. 21:28)

38. My son, _____ my voice. (Gen. 27:8)

39. O ye sons of _____. (Ps. 4:2)

41. And all that handle the _____. (Ezek. 27:29)

44. _____: and he smelleth the battle afar off. (Job 39:25)

35

PUZZLE 17

Lee Esch

ACROSS CLUES

1. The Son of man is come to save that which was _____. (Matt. 18:11)
5. Let down your _____ for a draught. (Luke 5:4)
9. Low-ranking soldier (abbr.).
12. Take thine _____, eat, drink and be merry. (Luke 12:19)
13. Lengthy, lyrical poems.
14. River (Spanish).
15. Metric unit.
16. Speaks of.
18. Blueprints.
20. Takes to court.
21. Grinned.
24. Frosted.
26. Ties (one's shoes).
27. Monotony.
30. A city in Oklahoma.
31. Setting.
33. That from which metal is extracted.
34. I would that all _____ _____ even as I myself. (1 Cor. 7:7; 2 words)
36. Stolen waters are _____. (Prov. 9:17)
38. Not my will, but thine, be _____. (Luke 22:42)
39. Thunderous rains.
40. _____ Stravinsky.
42. Small unclean animal. (Lev. 11:29)
44. Highway directories.
46. David dwelt in the _____. (2 Sam. 5:9)
50. For _____ have sinned. (Rom 3:23)
51. The home of Salt Lake City.
52. He came _____ his own. (John 1:11)

53. Major football organization (abbr.).
54. Sandwich shop.
55. Sly, suggestive look.

DOWN CLUES

1. Make bare the _____. (Isa. 47:2)
2. Boat paddle.
3. Social Security Administration (abbr.).
4. For the _____ of God is holy. (1 Cor. 3:17)
5. Desert wanderer.
6. God planted a garden eastward in _____. (Gen. 2:8)
7. Stress.
8. Supersonic transport (abbr.).
9. The Lord...plentifully rewardeth the _____ _____. (Ps. 31:23; 2 words)
10. I am the _____, ye are the branches. (John 15:5)
11. The waves thereof _____ themselves. (Isa. 5:22)
17. _____ _____ men as trees, walking. (Mark 8:24)
19. Diminish.
21. Close hard.
22. The word was _____ flesh. (John 1:14)
23. _____ _____ _____ _____ things through Christ. (Phil 4:13; 4 words)
25. Peaks.
27. For the _____ that is in the land of Assyria. (Isa. 7:18)
28. A city in Utah.
29. New York team.
32. Incinerate.
35. In the beginning was the _____. (John 1:1)
37. Neither have I desired the _____ day. (Jer. 17:16)

36

39. Japanese fish dish.
40. Tehran is its capital.
41. Country club sport.
43. Gem.
45. Wet dirt.

47. For there is _____ God. (Mark 12:32)
48. A fixed path of travel (abbr.).
49. Rocky hilltop.

PUZZLE 18

Lee Esch

ACROSS CLUES

1. Legislator. (abbr.).
4. But now is Christ risen from the _____. (1 Cor. 15:20)
8. For a good man some would even _____ to die. (Rom. 5:7)
12. There is none good but _____. (Matt. 19:17)
13. The Pharisees began to _____ him vehemently. (Luke 11:53)
14. Esau's other name. (Gen. 25:30)
15. National Institutes of Health. (abbr.).
16. Break sharply and quickly.
17. How unsearchable are his judgments, and his ways _____ finding out. (Rom. 11:33)
18. Fifth book of the Old Testament.
21. If I _____ touch but his clothes. (Mark 5:28)
22. Chronic drunkard.
23. Thou canst not make one _____ white or black. (Matt. 5:36)
25. Ye have made it a _____ of thieves. (Mark 11:17)
26. Be thou cast into the _____. (Mark 11:23)
29. A king of Judah. (1 Kgs. 15:9)
30. Dignity or composure.
32. Vase.
33. Miles per hour. (abbr.).
34. The beginning and the _____. (Rev. 21:6)
35. Small quarrel.
36. And all things _____ of God. (2 Cor. 5:18)
37. Company executive. (abbr.).
38. Is not this _____, _____ _____ of Joseph? (John 6:42; 3 words)
43. 100 centavos.
44. Sight-seeing trip.
45. The number of whom is as the sand of the _____. (Rev. 20:8)
47. A custard or fruit-filled tart.
48. Ova.
49. _____ tide.
50. Hint.
51. Sit for a photo.
52. Female deer.

DOWN CLUES

1. He that hath the _____ hath life. (1 John 5:12)
2. A city in Oklahoma.
3. The 16th book of the Old Testament.
4. Layered with dirt.
5. Sea eagle.
6. Mount Sinai. (Gal. 4:25)
7. Removes from position of power.
8. RR station.
9. The first man.
10. Pinkish.
11. Emergency Medical Technician (abbr.).
19. United Arab Republic (abbr.).
20. Silver and gold have I _____. (Acts 3:6)
23. Noah's second son. (Gen. 5:32)
24. Snake.
25. Therefore _____ the Jews persecute Jesus. (John 5:16)
26. They _____ it had been a spirit. (Mark 6:49)
27. Time period.
28. Go to the _____, thou sluggard. (Prov. 6:6)
30. South American country.

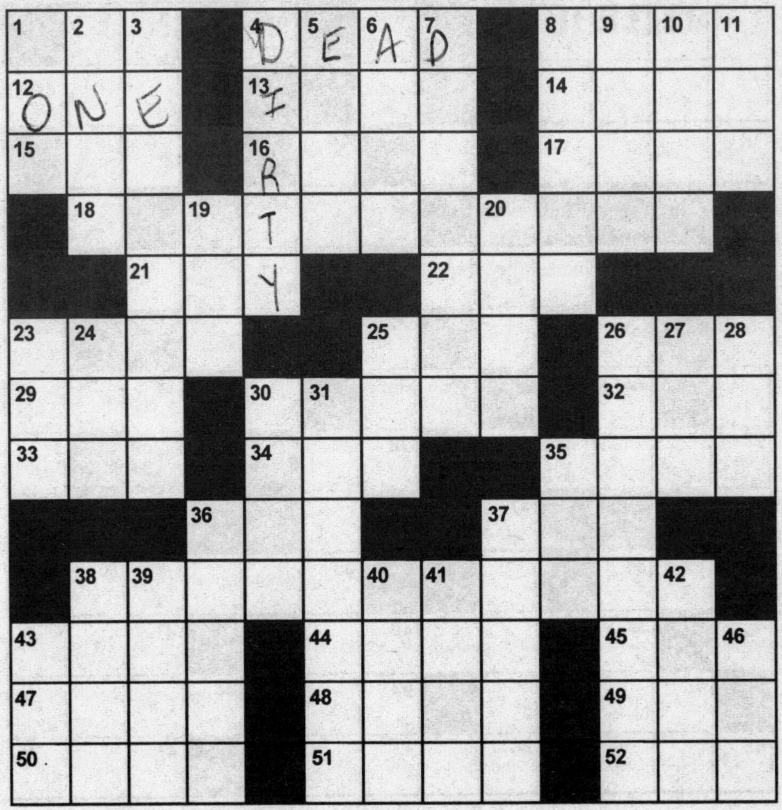

31. Ballroom dance.
35. Female sibling (abbr.).
36. Behold, the man is become _____ _____ of us. (Gen. 3:22; 2 words)
37. Poem division.
38. Congeal.
39. Isaac's oldest son. (Gen. 27:1)
40. He was afraid _____ _____ thither. (Matt. 2:22; 2 words)
41. Embraces.
42. Mountain where Moses died. (Deut. 32:49,50)
43. Private First Class (abbr.).
46. Pres. Lincoln's name (abbr.).

PUZZLE 19

Kathy Johnson

ACROSS CLUES

1. The name the angel called him. (Luke 2:21)
6. She bore a son, and called his name _____. (Gen. 4:25)
10. Why, what _____ hath he done? (Mark 15:14)
11. _____ of Tarsus. (Acts 9:11)
12. Cossack leader.
15. In the song, Jesus is _____ging on my heart strings.
16. The shorter version of the name Joshua.
18. The ninth book of the Old Testament.
20. The prophets prophesy _____ in my name. (Jer. 14:14)
22. When they saw the _____, they rejoiced. (Matt. 2:10)
23. _____, Lord! God! (Jer. 4:10)
25. _____ is the kingdom of God. (Mark 4:26)

26. Written not with _____, but with the Spirit. (2 Cor. 3:3)
27. This man denied Jesus three times.
29. East central state (abbr.).
31. The abbreviation for aluminum.
33. The first three letters of the alphabet.
35. _____ handmaid bare unto Abraham. (Gen. 25:12)
38. This woman was given to her husband as a reward for conquering a city. (Judg. 1:12)
41. A rodent.
42. My _____ is at hand. (Matt. 26:18)
43. It's not a he or a she, it's an _____.
44. Cast ballet.
45. All unrighteousness is _____. (1 John 5:17)
46. And a certain woman named _____, a seller of purple. (Acts 16:14)
47. No man putteth _____ wine into old bottles. (Luke 6:37)

DOWN CLUES

1. And _____ bowed his head. (2 Chron. 20:18)
2. Adam's wife.
3. _____ on my right hand. (Heb. 1:13)
4. A city in southwest Germany.
5. The opposite of *yes.*
7. The seventeenth book in the Old Testament.
8. The nineteenth letter in the Greek alphabet.
9. Very big.
13. Cain's brother.
14. Found the _____ tied by the door. (Mark 11:4)
17. Prefix meaning "saliva."
19. Fed you with milk, and not with _____. (1 Cor. 3:2)
21. Cursed is the ground for thy _____. (Gen. 3:17)
22. Reaping that I did not _____. (Luke 19:22)
24. _____ is not here. (Luke 24:6)
28. _____ had stolen the images. (Gen. 31:19)
30. This woman was banished by a king. (Es. 1)
32. And when _____ saw it, he built an altar before it. (Ex. 32:5)
34. The man who killed Abel.
36. Ye that love the Lord, _____ evil. (Ps. 97:10)
37. A type of soup.
39. The abbreviation of *centimeter.*
40. First _____ kit.
42. Seventh note.

PUZZLE 20

Janet W. Adkins

ACROSS CLUES

1. _____-a-brac.
5. Type of lettuce.
8. Canadian Indian tribe.
12. Sons of Benjamin... Ehi and ___.
(Gen. 46:21)
13. Mouth.
14. _____ avis; rarity.
15. Vapor (prefix).
16. Prominent sea (abbr.).
17. Company that tries harder.
18. The _____ of the righteous is only good. (Prov. 11:23)
20. And mine hand shall be upon the prophets...that _____ lies.
(Ezek. 13:9)
22. West Coast state (abbr.).
23. Greek letter.
24. _____ of errors.
27. That ye might be partakers of the divine _____. (2 Pet. 1:4)
31. Onassis.
32. Uncooked.
33. Orthodontist's product.
37. Death, and mourning, and _____.
(Rev. 18:8)
40. The name of the wicked shall _____. (Prov. 10:7)
41. Compass direction.
42. See that ye _____ not him that speaketh. (Heb. 12:25)
45. And I thank Christ Jesus our Lord, who hath _____(d) me.
(1 Tim. 1:12)
49. Ammihud, the son of _____.
(1 Chron. 9:4)
50. Priest's robe.
52. Platform.
53. Render therefore to all their _____.
(Rom. 13:7)
54. Bad (prefix).
55. Margarine.
56. This (Spanish).
57. South by east (abbr.).
58. A thready fragment.

DOWN CLUES

1. Nail with a small head.
2. Learning by repetition.
3. Belief systems (suffix).
4. God made _____ among us, that the Gentiles...should hear the gospel. (Acts 15:7)
5. Thy cheeks are _____ with rows of jewels. (Son of Sol. 1:10)
6. Mine product.
7. To cause dejection.
8. Tie.
9. River in India.
10. Ireland.
11. Take thine _____, eat, drink.
(Luke 12:19)
19. Radiation measure.
21. _____'s _____ boy!
24. The fourth part of a _____ of dove's dung. (2 Kgs. 6:25)
25. Hockey name Bobby _____.
26. _____ Farrow.
28. Geber the son of _____ was in the country of Gilead. (1 Kgs. 4:19)
29. His father saw him..._____, and fell on his neck. (Luke 15:20)
30. Poor man had nothing, save one little _____ lamb. (2 Sam. 12:3)
34. Ocean trip.
35. Greek goddess of the dawn.
36. Cooks vegetables.

37. Lift up the hands...and the _____ knees. (Heb. 12:12)
38. Girl's name.
39. A grassy field.
42. Past tense of *ride*.
43. Australian flightless birds.

44. They shall _____ themselves, and curse their king. (Is. 8:21)
46. Indonesian island.
47. Ye have eaten the fruit of _____. (Hosea 10:13)
48. Employee stock ownership plan.
51. Experiment room.

43

PUZZLE 21

Janet W. Adkins

ACROSS CLUES

1. Places of experiment.
5. It hath consumed ____ of Moab. (Num. 21:28)
7. Esau sold his birthright for ____.
11. Solomon's grandson. (1 Chron. 3:10)
12. Mother of Hezekiah. (2 Kgs. 18:12)
13. These ought ye to ____ done. (Matt. 23:23)
14. Woman's headwear.
16. And she [Shuah] conceived again and bore a son,... ____. (Gen. 38:4)
17. There remained two in the camp ...one was ____. (Num. 11:26)
18. Saul ____ his thousands, and David his ten thousands. (1 Sam. 29:5)
21. That escapeth from the sword of Jehu shall ____ slay. (1 Kgs. 19:17)
25. Military leader (abbr.).
28. For ye tithe mint and ____ and...herbs. (Luke 11:42)
30. Between (prefix).
31. Nicodemus...brought a mixture of myrrh and ____s. (John 19:39)
33. He that endureth to the ____ shall be saved. (Matt. 10:22)
35. V.P. Al ____.
36. Smallest.
38. And ____ orah a prophetess... judged Israel. (Judg. 4:4)
40. Ballet step (French).
41. Element.
43. Egg ____ yong.
45. Not with ____, as menpleasers. (Eph. 6:6)

50. Repetitive learning.
53. Not plural.
54. One thing on a list.
55. Telecommunications for the deaf (abbr.).
56. Optical device.
57. Puts on clothing.
58. Direction.
59. Soul, take thine ____. (Luke 12:19)

DOWN CLUES

1. And death and hell were cast unto the ____ of fire. (Rev. 20:14)
2. And the Lord had respect unto ____ and to his offering. (Gen. 4:4)
3. Their glory shall fly away like a ____. (Hosea 9:11)
4. Sons of Obed-edom... ____ the fourth. (1 Chron. 26:4)
5. Belonging to Abraham.
6. Firearm.
7. Displaying.
8. Sunbathe.
9. Madame Peron.
10. Cyst.
12. Joshua sent men from Jericho to ____. (Josh 7:2)
15. Head (abbr.).
19. Now the sons of ____ were sons of Belial. (1 Sam. 2:12)
20. Tribute to whom tribute is ____. (Rom. 13:7)
22. No man shall ____ me... (2 Cor. 11:10)
23. Greek goddess.
24. Greek god of war.
25. Young cow.
26. "Just as I am without one ____."
27. Turn over account (abbr.).

29. Whose _____ is destruction. (Phil. 3:19)
32. Regards highly.
34. The Lord of hosts shall _____ them. (Zech. 9:15)
37. Plaything.
39. Bjorn _____.
42. Relaxes.
44. Egg or droplet.

46. A thousand shall fall at thy _____. (Ps. 91:7)
47. Outer pelvic bones.
48. Storage vessels.
49. Gaelic.
50. That he might _____ him out of their hands. (Gen. 37:22)
51. Relating to the ear (prefix).
52. Give it unto him which hath _____ talents. (Matt. 25:28)

PUZZLE 22

Janet W. Adkins

ACROSS CLUES

1. Where Paul addressed the Athenians. (Acts 17:22)
8. Dull.
12. Short for Abraham.
13. The sons of _____; Arah, Haniel, and Rezia. (1 Chron. 7:39)
14. Take thine _____ eat, drink, and be merry. (Luke 12:19)
15. To them which were in _____. (1 Sam. 30:29)
17. Father of Isaac.
19. Belonging to a righteous king. (1 Kgs. 15:11)
20. And the _____ went and called the child's mother. (Ex. 2:8)
21. Nickname of Hephzibah.
22. Girl's name.
23. How dogs drink.
26. America.
29. Sons of Onam...Shammai, and _____. (1 Chron. 2:28)
30. Shalt not abhor an _____. (Deut. 23:7)
34. And _____, and Abimael, and Sheba. (Gen. 10:28)
35. Uncommon.
36. Mouth.
37. School subject (abbr.).
38. Rocky hill.
41. Cease.
45. Killer whale.
46. Let him eat at _____. (1 Cor. 11:34)
47. The vision of _____. (Obad. 1:1)
51. Retired (abbr.).
52. Courageous man.
53. The Dalai _____.
55. He is of _____; ask him. (John 9:21)
56. For we have seen his _____ in the east. (Matt. 2:2)
57. And he conferred...with _____ the priest. (1 Kgs. 1:7)

DOWN CLUES

1. They could not drink the waters of _____. (Ex. 15:23)
2. Those that walk in pride he is able to _____. (Dan. 4:37)
3. Rejuvenated auto tire.
4. And the children of Aram; Uz, and _____. (Gen. 10:23)
5. Negative prefix.
6. Andean best of burden.
7. Jacob's father-in-law. (Gen. 28:1-2)
8. Though he were _____, yet shall he live. (John 11:25)
9. A cheer.
10. _____ took the silver. (1 Kgs. 15:18)
11. Bachelor of engineering of mines (abbr.).
16. Suppose.
18. _____ Tin Tin.
23. Type of retriever (abbr.).
24. Woman's name.
25. Buddy.
27. Yes (Spanish).
28. _____ the name of Jesus every knee should bow. (Phil. 2:10)
29. An oak...that pertained unto _____. (Judg. 6:11)
30. The mother of all living. (Gen. 3:20)
31. From _____ even to Beer-sheba. (Judg. 20:1)
32. Organization (abbr.).

46

33. Hoshea...sent messengers to _____ king of Egypt. (2 Kgs. 17:4)
38. Prefix meaning "three."
39. Florida city.
40. By faith the harlot _____ perished not. (Heb. 11:31)
42. Jewish holy book.
43. I am Alpha and _____. (Rev. 1:8)
44. Then Simon _____ having a sword drew it. (John 18:10)
45. Smell.
47. _____ and ahs.
48. Wager.
49. Sons of Jether; Jephunneh, and Pispah, and _____. (1 Chron. 7:38)
50. Sheep's cry.
54. Musical note.

PUZZLE 23

Janet W. Adkins

ACROSS CLUES

1. Headwear.
4. Girl's name.
8. Delete (typesetter's term).
12. Genetic material.
13. French city.
14. Black (poetic).
15. _____ and outs.
16. Leaving us an example, that ye should follow his _____s. (1 Pet. 2:21)
17. Englishman.
18. Get up and about.
20. To chant.
22. Mine _____ is as nothing before thee. (Ps. 39:5)
23. Dove's sound.
24. We remember...the melons,...leeks, and the _____. (Num. 11:5)
27. The king's chamberlains, Bigthan and _____. (Es. 2:21)
31. Kinsman (abbr.).
32. Dessert.
33. Do not interpretations _____ to God? (Gen. 40:8)
37. Thy _____ shall be to thy husband. (Gen. 3:16)
40. Civil Aeronautics Authority. (abbr.).
41. Historical period.
42. Wager.
45. Elevated train.
46. Unoccupied.
50. The sons of Mushi; Mahli, and _____. (1 Chron. 23:23)
52. Hawaiian welcome presents.
54. Neither/_____.
55. Capital of Peru.
56. It is appointed unto men _____ to die. (Heb. 9:27)
57. Power maker.
58. Yet will they _____ upon the Lord. (Micah 3:11)
59. Edgar Allan's kin.
60. Whom do men _____ that I the Son of man am? (Matt. 16:13)

DOWN CLUES

1. Manger.
2. Queen _____ furniture.
3. As the flower of the grass he shall _____ away. (Jam. 1:10)
4. Every man shall pitch with the _____ of their father's house. (Num. 2:2)
5. As vinegar upon _____ (pl.), so is he that singeth songs to a heavy heart. (Prov. 25:20)
6. Frozen water.
7. Describe.
8. I am _____ both to the Greeks and ...Barbarians. (Rom. 1:14)
9. River in Spain.
10. Cut of meat.
11. Between (prefix).
19. Chinese religion.
21. As the days of _____. (Matt. 24:37)
24. Sphere.
25. Born.
26. Love worketh no _____ to his neighbour. (Rom. 13:10)
28. Upon, over (prefix).
29. _____, we would see Jesus. (John 12:21)
30. Part of a giggle.
34. In the work cited.

35. Scottish *no.*
36. Horse's gait.
37. Graven by art and man's _____. (Acts 17:29)
38. Expunges.
39. Internal pouch.
42. A _____ and a pomegranate. (Ex. 39:26)
43. Singer _____ Gorme.
44. Son of Ishmael. (Gen. 25:13-15)
47. The _____ are a people not strong. (Prov. 30:25)
48. A suddenly bright star.
49. Salver.
51. The herd _____ violently down steep place. (Luke 8:33)
53. _____ch walked with God: and he was not (Gen. 5:24)

PUZZLE 24

Janet W. Adkins

ACROSS CLUES

1. Indian tribe of Peru.
5. Turned to the land of _____ l. (1 Sam. 13:17)
9. Fuel.
12. Fly away like a _____. (Hosea 9:11)
13. Unwanted plant.
14. Form of *to be*.
15. A bright thought.
16. "Praise Jehovah."
18. The sin of Judah is written with...the point of a _____. (Jer. 17:1)
19. Form of medicine.
20. Symbol for tantalum.
21. Lawyer (abbr.).
22. Travel chest.
24. And their coast was from...all the kingdom of _____. (Josh. 13:30)
25. Women's patriotic organization.
28. Against me do they devise my _____. (Ps. 41:7)
29. Uncle (Spanish).
30. Soccer great.
31. Shoe width.
32. "Strength" (Heb.).
33. Christmas song.
34. Thou _____ the man. (2 Sam. 12:7)
36. Unusual occurrence.
37. Amasa was a man's son, whose name was _____. (2 Sam. 17:25)
40. Belonging to Ali.
41. The Lord is my _____. (Ps. 23:1)
43. And he came and touched the _____. (Luke 7:14)
46. Meadow.
47. Opera solo.
48. Company insignia.
49. Ever (poetic).
50. Malt beverage.
51. And Seth lived a hundred and five years, and begat _____. (Gen. 5:6)

DOWN CLUES

1. In the same place.
2. Nests.
3. Therefore if any man be in Christ, he is a new _____. (2 Cor. 5:17)
4. As an _____ harder than flint have I made thy forehead. (Ezek. 3:9)
5. Large white birds.
6. Retained.
7. Of the sons of Bani...Maadi, Amram, and _____. (Ezra 10:34)
8. Skilled.
9. Early France.
10. Seed covering.
11. For he hath founded it upon the _____. (Ps. 24:2)
17. Put flame to the candle.
21. The house that was builded these many years _____. (Ezra 5:11)
22. Article.
23. Ye tithe mint and _____ and herbs. (Luke 11:42)
24. He shall pour _____ upon it. (Lev. 2:1)
25. I am in _____ daily, everyone mocketh me. (Jer. 20:7)
26. Great amount (2 words).
27. Because thou didst _____ on the Lord. (2 Chron. 16:8)
29. Asian holiday.
30. Lord, speakest thou this _____ unto us. (Luke 12:41)
33. The fourth part of a _____ of dove's dung. (2 Kgs. 6:25)
34. Arpeggio (abbr.).

35. I will make mention of _____ and Babylon. (Ps. 87:4)
36. Detection device.
37. When they had gone through the _____ unto Paphos. (Acts 13:6)
38. Give his angels charge over _____. (Ps. 91:11)

39. _____, O Israel: The Lord our God is one Lord. (Deut. 6:4)
40. Type of cheese.
42. Before.
44. The self.
45. Mrs. Jimmy Carter.

PUZZLE 25

ACROSS CLUES

1. First person pronoun.
2. An insect abundant in Palestine. (Prov. 6:6)
4. A basket of _____ fruit. (Amos 8:2)
8. A negative reply .
9. Teach thee in the way which thou shalt _____. (Ps. 32:8)
10. In regard to.
11. Hebrew prophet swallowed by a great fish.
13. He made the _____ also. (Gen. 1:16)
14. To exist; to live.
15. Which is Christ in you, the _____ of glory. (Col. 1:27)
18. United States of America (abbr.).
20. Thou shalt not make unto thee any _____ image. (Ex. 20:4)
22. Be _____ your sin will find you out. (Num. 32:23)
24. Mary... _____ at Jesus' feet. (Luke 10:39)
25. A coarse file.
27. An aquatic carnivorous animal with flippers.
30. An exclamation of surprise.
32. I am the _____ of Sharon. (Song of Sol. 2:1)
33. Associated Press (abbr.).
35. _____, I am with you always. (Matt. 28:20)
36. Sign of God's covenant with Noah.
41. A prefix meaning "not."
42. Innings Pitched (abbr.).
43. An early king of Edom. (Gen. 36:37)
44. No man is _____ of life. (Job. 24:22)
45. Fire that _____ between *the* cherubims. (Ezek. 10:7)
46. Rosemary's nickname.
47. Neuter pronoun.
48. Neither too good nor too bad.
50. Hath _____ man condemned thee. (John 8:10)
51. They...came down to _____. (Acts 16:8)
52. The garden where Adam and Eve lived. (Gen. 2:8)

DOWN CLUES

1. Belonging to me.
2. Popular middle name for girl.
3. Man who built the ark. (Gen. 6)
4. _____ our eyes wait upon the Lord. (Ps. 123:2)
5. A female parent.
6. To sin.
7. Rephah was his son, also _____. (1 Chron. 7:25)
11. God's son.
12. Pigs.
14. Vehicle for public conveyance of passengers.
16. We commune with God through _____.
17. Man did _____ angels' food. (Ps. 78:25)
19. Ye _____ a chosen generation. (1 Pet. 2:9)
21. Symbol for sodium.
23. First.
26. Sung by one person.
28. Ring.
29. To the seven churches which are in _____. (Rev. 1:4)
31. A dried grape. (1 Sam. 25:18)
34. The planet farthest from the sun.

52

37. Took away the sheep, and the oxen, and the _____. (1 Sam. 27:9)
38. Deborah was Rebckah's _____. (Gen. 35:8)
39. Without shedding of _____ is no remission. (Heb. 9:22)
40. Four-wheeled vehicle.
45. _____ will have all men to be saved. (1 Tim. 2:4)
49. Southeast (abbr.).

PUZZLE 26

Pamela Jensen

ACROSS CLUES

1. All things work together for _____.
   (Rom. 8:28)
5. Thou shalt be a _____. (Gen. 12:2)
12. Provoke not your children to _____.
    (Col. 3:21)
14. Capably.
15. The Lord _____ high is mightier.
    (Ps. 93:4)
16. And _____ her head. (2 Kgs. 9:30)
17. His deadly _____ was healed.
    (Rev. 13:3)
18. Weeded, cultivated.
20. National Recovery Administration
    (abbr.).
21. _____ the time appointed.
    (Gen. 18:14)
22. Ensign (abbr.).
23. He _____ is my rock. (Ps. 62:2)
25. A precious stone.
27. Royal Society (abbr.).
28. Vigor, strength.
29. For our lamps are _____ out.
    (Matt. 25:8)
30. Sent men from Jericho to _____.
    (Josh. 7:2)
31. Indicates three.
33. Earns, gains.
35. _____, thou art the Son of God.
    (John 1:49)
38. Turned into the _____ of summer.
    (Ps. 32:4)
40. Spirit of adoption, whereby we cry,
    _____. (Rom. 8:15)
41. Because thou didst _____ on the
    Lord. (2 Chron. 16:8)
42. A period of time.
43. Perhaps, possibly.

45. Let him _____. (Jam. 1:6)
47. Learn to _____ well. (Is. 1:17)
49. Shall we _____ with the sword?
    (Luke 22:49)
51. He that shall _____ unto the end.
    (Mark 13:13)
55. I _____ the door. (John 10:9)
56. Have _____ to righteousness.
    (Rom. 9:30)
57. The Lord stirred _____ the spirit.
    (Ezra 1:1)

DOWN CLUES

1. A _____ of sycamore fruit.
   (Amos 7:14)
2. Leeks, and the _____, and the
   garlick. (Num. 11:5)
3. Fabled giants.
4. But in _____ and in truth.
   (1 John 3:18)
6. Sin is the transgression of the
   _____. (1 John 3:4)
7. Horns of ivory and _____.
   (Ezek. 27:15)
8. To pronounce indistinctly.
9. I ever taught in the _____.
   (John 18:20)
10. Do thyself _____ harm. (Acts 16:28)
11. Strain at a _____. (Matt. 23:24)
13. Rural Delivery (abbr.).
19. An individual part of a whole.
21. A ligure, an agate, and an _____.
    (Ex. 39:12)
23. We live therefore, _____ die.
    (Rom. 14:8)
24. Butter in a _____ dish. (Judg. 5:25)
26. From Engedi even unto _____.
    (Ezek. 47:10)
28. A bracket on the ship's mast to
    support the trestle trees.
30. He said, _____, Father.
    (Mark. 14:36)

32. Symbol for element iridium.
34. Saint (abbr.).
36. He will bless the house of _____.
    (Ps. 115:12)
37. But whom say ye that _____ _____?
    (Mark 8:29; 2 words)
39. Minerals from which metals can be
    mined.
42. The garden of _____. (Joel 2:3)

44. Height times width.
46. _____ yourselves in the love of
    God. (Jude 21)
48. _____ it also in writing. (Ezra 1:1)
50. The nations are _____. (Jer. 51:7)
52. District Attorney (abbr.).
53. Right (abbr.).
54. And it shall come to pass _____ the
    last days. (Isa. 2:2)

PUZZLE 27

Pamela Jensen

ACROSS CLUES

1. _____, and be not afraid.
   (Matt. 17:7)
5. Be of good _____. (Isa. 41:6)
11. I will bless her, and _____ thee a
    son. (Gen. 17:16)
12. I will _____ all the families.
    (Jer. 1:15)
13. American Library Association.
    (abbr.).
14. Symbol for element rubidium.
15. Every man according to his _____.
    (Acts 11:29)
17. The kingdom of _____ in Bashan.
    (Josh. 13:12)
18. Salah begat _____. (Gen. 10:24)
19. Airport code for Tel Aviv/Jaffa,
    Israel.
20. British rank above a viscount and
    below a marquis.
21. Ex officio (abbr.).
22. A small, low islet of coral or sand.
24. Extravehiclular activity (abbr.).
26. Turn _____ unto me. (Zech. 1:3)
27. Minnesota (abbr.).
28. _____ shall offer it. (Lev. 1:3)
30. The _____ of the Lord. (John 12:38)
33. Capital of South Korea.
36. Play on the hole of the _____.
    (Is. 11:8)
39. And _____ is the way. (Matt. 7:14)
42. Daughters shall be _____. (Is. 60:4)
44. A company or group.
45. A group of five.
46. One _____ without blemish.
    (Num. 6:14)
47. Master of Arts (abbr.).

49. Eleazar the son of _____.
    (2 Sam. 23:9)
50. Eight quarts.
51. For the sky is _____. (Matt. 16:2)
53. Actual Weight (abbr.).
54. Large open Eskimo boat.
56. I come to _____ thy will.
    (Heb. 10:9)
57. Monsignor (abbr.).
58. The Lord is _____ hand. (Joel 1:15)
59. The patience of _____. (Jam. 5:11)

DOWN CLUES

1. Make an _____ with me. (Is. 36:16)
2. A narrow strip of fabric.
3. Intravenous (abbr.).
4. _____ me...and know my heart.
   (Ps. 139:23)
5. Whosoever shall _____ on the
   name. (Acts 2:21)
6. In her mouth was an _____ leaf.
   (Gen. 8:11)
7. Ultimate (abbr.).
8. Associate in Arts (abbr.).
9. To him be _____. (Rev. 1:6)
10. He shall fly as an _____.
    (Jer. 48:40)
12. In the _____ of David. (Luke 2:4)
16. To Jerusalem every _____.
    (Luke 2:41)
23. Sixth century B.C. Greek author of
    fables.
25. Of more _____ than many spar-
    rows. (Luke 12:7)
29. I will not _____ it. (Gen. 18:30)
31. Ye also have a _____ in heaven.
    (Col. 4:1)
32. _____ is the way. (Matt. 7:13)
34. One little _____ lamb.
    (2 Sam. 12:3)
35. To remove the contents.

37. _____ with that holy Spirit of promise. (Eph. 1:13)
38. Doctor of Pedagogy (abbr.).
40. Sharp _____ of the mighty. (Ps. 120:4)
41. I have heard a _____ from the Lord. (Jer. 49:14)
43. Registered Nurse (abbr.).

47. All eat the same spiritual _____. (1 Cor. 10:3)
49. Seven days under the _____. (Lev. 22:27)
50. Airport code for Peoria, Illinois.
52. Female deer.
55. Now it came _____ pass. (Ruth 1:1)

PUZZLE 28

Pamela Jensen

ACROSS CLUES

1. Be ye kind one to another, _____.
   (Eph. 4:32)
12. O Lord, _____ me. (Ps. 6:2)
13. _____, thou art the Son of God.
    (John 1:49)
15. In Christ shall all be made _____.
    (1 Cor. 15:22)
17. National Basketball Association
    (abbr.).
18. Slippery.
19. A righteous man hateth _____.
    (Prov. 13:5)
21. The Hushathite slew _____.
    (2 Sam. 21:18)
23. Kentucky (abbr.).
25. Georgia (abbr.).
26. Enos, which was the son of _____.
    (Luke 3:38)
28. As the sand which is by the _____.
    (Heb. 11:12; 2 words)
30. Part of an ephah of barley _____.
    (Num. 5:15)
32. The prophet _____, David's seer.
    (2 Sam. 24:11)
33. Symbol for element thulium.
34. Veterans' Administration (abbr.).
36. God called the light _____.
    (Gen. 1:5)
37. And _____, and Migdal-el.
    (Josh. 19:38)
39. A single article.
41. Emergency Room (abbr.).
42. Cast the _____ on the right side.
    (John 21:6)
44. I will make of thee _____ great
    _____. (Gen. 12:2; 2 words.
46. _____ took Jeremiah. (Jer. 37:14)

49. Will set fire in _____. (Ezek. 30:14)
50. Should tell _____ man. (Luke 8:56)
51. Gone down in the _____.
    (2 Kgs. 20:11)
53. Ephesians (abbr.).
55. _____ will establish it for ever.
    (Ps. 48:8)
57. Make bare the _____. (Isa. 47:2)
58. District Attorney (abbr.).
59. _____ found a ship going to
    Tarshish. (Jonah 1:3)
60. Why will ye go with _____?
    (Ruth 1:11)
61. The bright and morning _____.
    (Rev. 22:16)
62. The _____ of the Lord. (Isa. 9:7)

DOWN CLUES

1. Magnify him with _____.
   (Ps. 69:30)
2. Long, snakelike fish.
3. She put her hand to the _____.
   (Judg. 5:26)
4. Delivery (abbr.).
5. Railroad (abbr.).
6. And they shall _____ upon him.
   (Isa. 22:24)
7. To fall back or recede.
8. Walk in pride he is able to _____.
   (Dan. 4:37)
9. Rhode Island (abbr.).
10. And peace have kissed _____ other.
    (Ps. 85:10)
11. The sun to rule by _____.
    (Ps. 136:8)
16. Isaac being _____ days old.
    (Gen. 21:4
18. And _____, and Penuel.
    (1 Chron. 8:25)
20. There is a son born to _____.
    (Ruth 4:17)

58

22. Atmosphere (abbr.).

24. A day, and a month, and a _____. (Rev. 9:15)

26. _____ men of honest report. (Acts 6:3)

27. A town in eastern England.

29. When _____-zede king of Jerusa-lem. (Josh 10:1)

31. He will bless the house of _____. (Ps. 115:12)

35. And they were all _____. (Luke 4:36)

38. Province of Saudi Arabia.

40. Symbol for element tantalum.

43. There were stings in their _____. (Rev. 9:10)

45. The _____ of Ethiopia shall not equal it. (Job 28:19)

47. They went up into an upper _____. (Acts 1:13)

48. A minute amount (Scot.).

52. Airport code for La Guardia, New York.

54. I will punish _____. (Jer. 51:44)

56. Delaware (abbr.).

59. Interjection expressing derision.

PUZZLE 29

Rebecca Souder

ACROSS CLUES

1. Brotherly _____. (2 Pet. 1:7)
8. Cuts of meat.
9. Grace and _____ be multiplied. (2 Pet. 1:2)
13. Through the _____ of him that hath called us. (2 Pet. 1:3)
16. Charged particle.
17. Jupiter's moon.
18. Overdose (abbr.).
19. Explosive.
21. Eschew evil, and do _____. (1 Pet. 3:11)
23. Exclamation.
24. _____ and peace be multiplied. (2 Pet. 1:2)
27. Evil plan.
29. South America (abbr.).
30. That ye might be partakers of the _____ nature. (2 Pet. 1:4)
32. If these things be _____ you. (2 Pet. 1:8)
33. This is my beloved _____. (2 Pet. 1:17)
34. Poem.
35. Family group.
37. Greek letter.
38. Manuscript (abbr.).
39. And to knowledge _____. (2 Pet. 1:6)
41. Puerto Rico (abbr.).
42. Old style (abbr.).
43. Thou shalt make the _____ of the tabernacle. (Ex. 27:9)
46. Our _____ Jesus Christ.
50. Add to your faith _____. (2 Pet. 1:5)
51. _____, I am with you always. (Matt. 28:20)
52. Tin (symbol).
53. _____ _____ God gave unto them. (Acts 11:17 ASV; 2 words)
54. His divine _____ hath given unto us. (2 Pet. 1:3)

DOWN CLUES

2. Labor organization (abbr.).
3. Beloved, _____ are we the sons of God. (1 John 3:2)
4. Besides this, giving all _____, add to your faith virtue. (2 Pet. 1:5)
5. Direction.
6. Apocryphal book Esdras (abbr.).
7. Went quickly.
11. Convict (abbr.).
12. For so an _____ shall be. (2 Pet. 1:11)
13. Into the everlasting _____. (2 Pet. 1:11)
14. That _____ prophecy of the scripture. (2 Pet. 1:20)
15. All things that pertain unto life and _____. (2 Pet. 1:3)
20. Doth also now _____ us. (1 Pet. 3:21)
22. Out of print (abbr.).
23. I fell _____ his feet as dead. (Rev. 1:17)
25. Eliminates.
26. 101 (Roman).
28. With him _____ the sacred mountain. (2 Pet. 1:18 NIV)
29. For _____ an entrance shall be. (2 Pet. 1:11)
31. Tree.
33. He was purged from his old _____s. (2 Pet. 1:9)
36. Military address.

37. Ma's mate.
39. Be established in the present _____.
    (2 Pet. 1:12)
40. I _____ you...to go and bear fruit.
    (John 15:16 NIV)
41. Sea _____.
43. Cost, insurance and freight (abbr.).
44. Regret.
45. Likened unto _____ virgins.
    (Matt. 25:1)
47. European mountain.
48. ___doo, African sorcery.
49. Royal Naval Reserve (abbr.).
50. 6 (Roman).

PUZZLE 30

Rebecca Souder

ACROSS CLUES

1. Greek letter.
3. Being the _____ of his glory. (Heb. 1:3)
11. One who inherits (2 words).
13. Greek monogram for Jesus.
14. Pint (abbr.).
15. And the... _____ of his person. (Heb. 1:3)
16. To whom shall we _____? (John. 6:68)
17. Either/_____.
18. Headquarters (abbr.).
19. New Hampshire.
20. _____ saith the Lord.
21. Kansas University.
22. New wine will _____ the bottles. (Luke. 5:37)
24. His servants _____ him. (John. 4:51)
25. That is (Latin abbr.).
26. French coin.

28. Thirty silver _____. (Matt. 26:15 NIV)
29. Greek vowel.
30. Better.
32. Comb. form meaning "wood."
33. _____ all things by the word of his power. (Heb. 1:3)
36. Thy throne, O God, _____ for ever. (Heb. 1:8)
37. A division of Scripture.
38. ...art my _____. (Heb. 1:5)
39. Grain or bread.
42. A more excellent _____ than they. (Heb. 1:4)
45. Greek porch.
46. Greek goddess.
47. Shew you a more _____ way. (1 Cor. 12:31)
49. Storekeeper (abbr.).
50. _____ hospitality one to another. (1 Pet. 4:9)
51. He that hath an _____ let him hear. (Rev. 2:7)
52. Kind of worshipers the Father _____. (Jn 4:23 NIV)
53. He looked for a _____. (Heb. 11:10)

DOWN CLUES

1. Ma's mate.
2. Hated _____. (Heb. 1:9)
3. Vegetables.
4. Loved _____. (Heb. 1:9)
5. Anger.
6. Right hand of the Majesty on _____. (Heb. 1:3)
7. _____ art my Son. (Heb. 1:5)
8. Nova Scotia (abbr.).
9. Hath in these last days _____ unto us. (Heb. 1:2)
10. Walks proudly.
12. His Majesty (abbr.).
18. Hemoglobin (abbr.).
20. The word of _____. (Jam. 1:18)
23. True.
24. Sent forth to _____ for them who shall be heirs of salvation. (Heb. 1:14)
27. Drink this ___. (1 Cor. 11:26)
28. Sitting upon...a _____. (Matt. 21:5)
29. And the _____...of his person. (Heb. 1:3)
31. Recipient.
34. Come nigh unto Damascus about _____. (Acts 22:6)
35. Dust...became _____. (Ex. 8:17 NIV)
40. My _____ is easy. (Matt. 11:30)
41. Emergency Service (abbr.).
43. The _____ is laid the root. (Matt. 3:10)
44. Master of Ceremonies (abbr.).
45. I will _____ thy son. (Ex. 4:23)
48. _____ there be light. (Gen. 1:3)
50. United Kingdom (abbr.).

PUZZLE 31

Connie Holman

ACROSS CLUES

1. Are they _____? (2 Cor. 11:22)
8. Pronoun for male.
10. There hath _____ temptation taken you. (1 Cor. 10:13)
11. Move laboriously.
12. A flattering mouth worketh _____. (Prov. 26:28)
13. Precious stone.
14. Athaliah the daughter of _____. (2 Chron. 22:2)
17. Second note of musical scale.
18. Good works for necessary _____. (Titus 3:14)
19. Death shall _____ from them. (Rev. 9:6)
20. Garment edge.
22. Opposite of came.
24. *Yes* in Spanish.
25. Selenium (abbr.).
26. His only _____ son. (John 3:16)
28. Work.
29. _____ the hart panteth. (Ps. 42:1)
30. Father.
32. Times when sun is farthest north or south in the ecliptic.
35. Do not set up any wooden _____ pole. (Deut. 16:21, NIV)
37. You.
38. _____ de Janeiro.
39. A tropical bird.
40. Three measures of barley for a _____. (Rev. 6:6)
42. I am ashamed and _____. (Ezra 9:6)
44. Yellowish green fruit.
46. _____ ye even so to them. (Matt.7:12)

47. Too.
49. _____ him were all things created. (Col. 1:16)
50. Belonging to a female.
51. Type of grain.
52. Pierces.
53. For we _____ his workmanship. (Eph. 2:10)

DOWN CLUES

1. Brings upon himself.
2. Therefore.
3. Silver, ivory, and _____. (1 Kings 10:22)
4. Type of shade tree.
5. And, _____, I am with you. (Matt. 28:20)
6. Honoring false gods.
7. _____ Lanka.
8. All the _____ thereof shall be burned. (Micah 1:7)
9. Make thine _____ thy footstool. (Heb. 1:13)
13. Acquire.
15. An help _____ for him. (Gen. 2:18)
16. Veil of the temple was _____. (Mark 15:38)
21. Israel's female judge.
23. Apostle, and a _____ of the Gentiles. (2 Tim. 1:11)
26. _____ things of the world. (1 Cor. 1:28)
27. _____ in Bashan. (Deut. 4:43)
29. They were sawn _____. (Heb. 11:37)
30. At _____ westward. (1 Chron. 26:18)
31. Like _____ dove. (Hosea 7:11; 2 words)
33. Worth doing (2 words).
34. Very long time.

36. Built his _____ upon a rock.
    (Matt. 7:24)
41. Time long past.
43. _____ shall we ever be with the
    Lord. (1 Thes. 4:17)

45. Decline.
48. Location.
50. Expression of triumph.

PUZZLE 32

Connie Holman

ACROSS CLUES

1. Thou shalt plant _____.
   (Deut. 28:39)
8. Standeth in _____ of thy word.
   (Ps. 119:161)
11. House _____ God. (Gen. 28:17)
12. More recent.
13. Once more; in a different way.
14. Scottish language.
16. Let your communication _____,
    Yea, yea. (Matt. 5:37)
17. Opposite of over.
19. Bays or coves.
22. Have _____ other gods before me.
    (Ex. 20:3)
23. Give to him that _____.
    (Matt. 5:42)
24. Characteristic.
27. Thou art _____ great. (Ps. 104:1)
28. Nothing more than.
30. Gather the _____ of Israel.
    (Ex. 3:16)
33. Stubborn.

34. More uncommon.
35. _____ lib.
36. Heavenly.
39. A time to rend, and a time to _____.
    (Ec. 3:7)
40. Nay.
41. My days _____ fulfilled.
    (Gen. 29:21)
43. Courtyard.
45. Trodden under foot of _____.
    (Matt. 5:13)
46. In the middle of.
47. The hearts of the people _____.
    (Josh. 7:5)

DOWN CLUES

1. One who works freely.
2. _____ my people, which are called by my name. (2 Chron. 7:14)
3. In the wilderness of _____.
    (1 Sam. 24:1)
4. _____ of jubilee. (Lev. 27:17)
5. Stand in _____, and sin not.
    (Ps. 4:4)
6. Take pleasure in.
7. Neither eat nor _____. (Es. 4:16)
8. _____ angel of the Lord.
    (Luke 1:11)

9. Spider homes.
10. Save one little _____ lamb.
    (2 Sam. 12:3)
15. Cunning.
18. Thou, _____, thy son. (Ex. 20:10)
20. But the righteous into life _____.
    (Matt. 25:46)
21. Number of Noah's sons. (Gen 6:10)
25. Brother of Simon Peter.
26. Raging floods.
28. Small amount.
29. Breach for breach, _____ for _____.
    (Lev. 24:20)
31. Put it on a blue _____. (Ex 28:37)
32. Snakelike fish.
35. _____ home in the body.
    (2 Cor. 5:6)
37. Every bird of every _____.
    (Gen 7:14)
38. Eat of the _____ of life. (Rev 2:7)
39. Resort area; gym.
41. Quantity (abbr.).
42. The _____ of all things is at hand.
    (1 Pet. 4:7)
43. In the year of our Lord.
44. As for _____ and my house.
    (Josh. 24:15)

PUZZLE 33

Connie Holman

ACROSS CLUES

1. Your _____ shall be desolate. (Ezek 6:4)
6. They had made themselves _____ to David. (1 Chron. 19:6)
11. Overshoe.
12. _____ and void.
13. Lose his life for my sake shall find _____. (Matt.16:25)
14. Affectedly shy.
16. Thicker parts at ends of side walls.
17. Being _____ freely by his grace. (Rom. 3:24)
20. _____, ego, superego.
21. _____ for me and my house. (Josh. 24:15)
22. Hoax.
24. Being _____ by the Holy Ghost. (Rom. 15:16)
28. _____ the son of Nun. (Num. 13:8)
29. Behold, all things are become _____. (2 Cor. 5:17)
30. Pass through the fire to _____. (2 Kgs. 23:10)
31. Anger.
33. Crack in a container.
34. Behind a vessel.
36. _____ the son of Abdiel. (1 Chron. 5:15)
38. A _____ of dragons. (Jer. 9:11)
40. Child.
41. With the same measure that ye _____. (Luke 6:38)
43. I _____ set my bow in the cloud. (Gen. 9:13)
44. Wing of building.
46. Primp.
48. _____ Syndrome.
50. For God _____ loved the world. (John 3:16)
51. Which is _____ in the scripture. (Dan. 10:21)
52. _____ gave his only begotten Son. (John 3:16)

DOWN CLUES

1. _____ the son of Jeroboam. (1 Kgs. 14:1)
2. Aquatic plant.
3. Light _____ rule the day. (Gen. 1:16)
4. I stand _____ the door. (Rev. 3:20)
5. Behold, it is a _____ people. (Ex. 32:9)
6. Potipherah priest of _____. (Gen. 46:20)
7. No room for them in the _____. (Luke 2:7)
8. There went _____ a decree from Caesar Augustus. (Luke 2:1)
9. I was by the river of _____. (Dan. 8:2)
10. Winter coasting vehicle.
14. Third note of musical scale.
15. Nahor's wife. (Gen. 11:29)
16. Have charge of, manage.
18. Scuffle.
19. They did all _____, and were filled. (Matt. 14:20)
23. Every 14 days.
25. Yet to come.
26. Able to reproduce.
27. Mend a stocking.
28. Limestone.
32. There were seven of _____ fire. (Rev. 4:5)
35. Second note of musical scale.

37. Great man.
39. I will not put my hook in thy _____.
    (2 Kgs. 19:28)
42. Even (contraction).

45. When ye pray, _____ not vain
    repetitions. (Matt. 6:7)
47. Thy servants have _____ pasture.
    (Gen. 47:4)
49. What?

PUZZLE 34

Teresa Zeek

ACROSS CLUES

1. Seek ye the Lord while he may be _____. (Isa. 55:6)
5. Go and _____ no more. (John 8:11)
8. In the beginning _____. (Gen. 1:1)
11. When we come to the _____. (Gen. 43:21)
12. In Gaza, in Gath, and in _____. (Josh. 11:22)
15. The second tone of the diatonic scale.
16. Cunning in knowledge, and understanding _____. (Dan. 1:4)
18. University of Iowa (abbr.).
19. Pennsylvania (abbr.).
20. Son of Canaan. (Gen. 10:15)
21. O come let us _____ Him.
22. God, who _____ sundry times. (Heb. 1:1)
23. And the tree of the field shall _____ her fruit. (Eze. 34:27)
24. An exclamation of relief.
25. Road (abbr.).
27. The power of _____ and Media. (Es. 1:3)
29. Heard me out of his holy hill. _____. (Ps. 3:4)
33. Another name for Mt. Sinai. (Deut. 4:10)
36. Christ _____ in me. (Gal. 2:20)
38. Thy will be _____ in earth. (Matt. 6:10)
39. White starchy grain.
40. It will _____ (s) him to powder. (Luke 20:18)
42. Shall bake your bread in one _____. (Lev. 26:26)

43. Borrow money take _____ _____. (2 words)
45. Southeast (abbr.).
46. To day shalt thou _____ with me in paradise. (Luke 23:43)
47. Paul studied at the feet of _____. (Acts 22:3)
50. Who concerning the truth have _____. (2 Tim. 2:18)
52. In the beginning _____ the word. (John 1:1)
53. A well from which Jacob called Abner. (2 Sam. 3:26)
54. Baruch's father. (Jer. 32:12)

DOWN CLUES

1. I will make you _____ of men. (Mark 1:17)
2. It is appointed unto men _____ to die. (Heb. 9:27)
3. Endeavoring to keep the _____ of the Spirit. (Eph. 4:3)
4. A son of Jacob by Bilhah. (Gen. 30:5,6)
5. Whoso _____ man's blood, by man shall his blood be shed. (Gen. 9:6)
6. Identification (abbr.).
7. I will _____ you, and your little ones. (Gen. 50:21)
9. Naomi's daughter-in-law. (Ruth 1:14)
10. _____ is swallowed up in victory. (1 Cor. 15:54)
13. God shall wound the...hairy _____. (Ps. 68:21)
14. Blessed are the dead which _____ in the Lord. (Rev. 14:13)
17. One of the sons of Benjamin. (Gen. 46:21)
24. Moses' brother. (Ex. 4:14)

26. The angel of the Lord encamps round about them that fear him, and _____ them. (Ps. 34:7 NKJV)
28. A nonmetallic chemical element used in medicine.
30. The third plague. (Ex. 8:16)
31. Still the enemy and the _____. (Ps. 8:2)
32. _____ restoreth my soul. (Ps. 23:3)
34. He shall be great unto the _____ of the earth. (Micah. 5:4)
35. I _____ you therefore, brethren. (Rom 12:1)
37. A group of people playing together.
39. Jonathan stripped himself of the _____. (1 Sam. 18:4)
40. One of the cities of refuge. (Deut. 4:43)
41. The Lord shall _____ him up. (Jam. 5:15)
44. It is written in the _____ of Moses. (1 Kgs. 2:3)
48. A woman's name.
49. A garland of flowers.
51. Rhode Island (abbr.).

71

PUZZLE 35

Teresa Zeek

ACROSS CLUES

1. Balaam's father. (Num. 22:5)
5. God the Father and in the _____ Jesus Christ. (1 Thes. 1:1)
9. _____ Lord bless thee. (Num. 6:24)
12. Mine _____ is kindled against them. (Hosea 8:5)
14. One of Caleb's sons. (1 Chron. 4:15)
16. A suffix used to form certain plurals.
17. I fell _____ his feet as dead. (Rev. 1:17)
18. Joshua sent men from Jericho to _____. (Josh. 7:2)
19. They removed from Jotbathah and encamped at _____. (Num. 33:34)
21. And _____ us not into temptation. (Matt. 6:13.)
24. Hadad's father. (Gen. 36:35)
25. Nickname for Raymond.
26. King (French).
28. Wise men come from the _____. (Matt. 2:1)
31. The Lord is _____ indeed. (Luke 24:34)
33. A suffix meaning "devotion to."
34. Joab saw that the _____ of the battle was against him. (2 Sam. 10:9)
36. _____ therefore, having your loins girt about with truth. (Eph. 6:14)
38. Jesus wrote on the ground with his _____. (John 8:6)
40. _____ let the wickedness of the wicked come to an end. (Ps. 7:9)
41. _____ man cometh unto the Father, but by me. (John 14:6)
42. Identification (abbr.).

43. Every man having his _____ in his hand. (2 Chron. 23:10)
45. _____ good to them that hate you. (Matt. 5:44)
47. Jesus' name for Simon meaning "stone." (John 1:42)
49. Nickname for Donald.
51. If any of you do _____ from the truth. (Jam. 5:19)
52. And they put on him a purple _____. (John 19:2)
55. The unit of electromotive force.
57. Simon Peter's brother. (Matt. 4:18)
58. Aholibamah's mother. (Gen. 36:14)
59. The evening and the morning were the first _____. (Gen. 1:5)
60. The herd ran down a _____ place. (Luke 8:33)
61. Editors (abbr.).

DOWN CLUES

1. A son of Joel. (1 Chron. 5:45)
2. _____ into his gates with thanksgiving. (Ps. 100:4)
3. The King of Bashan. (Num. 21:33)
4. Preparing.
6. Bear ye _____ another's burdens. (Gal. 6:12)
7. Title interpreted as *Master*. (John 1:38)
8. For a good man some would even _____ to die. (Rom. 5:7)
10. The seven _____ are seven mountains. (Rev. 17:9)
11. One of Saul's sons, _____-baal. (1 Chron. 8:33)
13. Rhode Island (abbr.).
15. That women adorn themselves in _____ apparel. (1 Tim. 2:9)
20. Captain of the host of the King of Syria; leper. (2 Kgs. 5:1)
22. Moses' brother. (Ex. 4:14)
23. Blessed _____ the meek. (Matt. 5:5)

27. That no _____ of you be puffed up. (1 Cor. 4:6)
29. A little child (esp. a boy).
30. The _____ of a midwife. (Ex. 1:16)
32. As good _____ of the manifold grace of God. (1 Pet. 4:10)
33. Hammoleketh's son. (1 Chron. 7:18)
35. I will break in pieces the chariot and his _____. (Jer. 51:21)
37. Cain dwelt in the land of _____. (Gen. 4:16)
39. _____ ye thither unto us. (Neh. 4:20)
40. A style of abstract painting creating optical illusions.
44. A star that brightens intensely and then gradually dims.
46. Perform unto the Lord thine _____. (Matt. 5:33)
48. He departed into a mountain to _____. (Mark 6:46)
50. For _____ of us liveth to himself. (Rom. 14:7)
53. The Lord shall hiss...for the _____ that is in the land. (Isa. 7:18)
54. The poor man had nothing save one little _____ lamb. (2 Sam. 12:3)
56. There is a _____ here, which hath five barley loaves. (John 6:9)

PUZZLE 36

Teresa Zeek

ACROSS CLUES

1. What the children of Israel ate for forty years. (Ex. 16:35)
6. There hath _____ temptation taken you. (1 Cor. 10:13)
8. The firstborn of Isaac's twin sons. (Gen. 25:25)
11. Joel and Jehu's great-grandfather. (1 Chron. 4:35)
12. Shuah's second son. (Gen. 38:24)
14. Southern state (abbr.).
15. _____ and see that the Lord is good. (Ps. 34:8)
16. We were comforted over you in _____ our affliction. (1 Thes. 3:7)
17. The voice of _____ crying in the wilderness. (Matt. 1:3)
18. _____ for me and my house, we will serve the Lord. (Josh. 24:15)
19. _____ kingdom come. (Matt. 6:10)
20. Herod slew the children... _____ years old and under. (Matt. 2:16)
21. Even as a _____ gathereth her chickens under her wings. (Matt. 23:37)
23. The fourth tone of the diatonic scale.
24. A prophetess, the daughter of Panuel. (Luke 2:36)
26. A suffix forming the comparative degree.
27. God _____ forth his Son. (Gal. 4:4)
29. Mister (abbr.).
30. Moses _____ all the words of the Lord. (Ex. 24:4)
32. King of the Amalekites. (1 Sam. 15:8)
34. Street (abbr.).
35. One of the children of Shobal. (Gen. 36:23)
36. The well, Beer-lahai-roi, is between _____ and Bered. (Gen. 16:14)

38. And Zebadiah, and Arad, and _____. (1 Chron. 8:15)
39. I will punish _____ in Babylon. (Jer. 51:44)
40. At _____ time. (Matt. 12:1)
42. _____ though I walk through the valley. (Ps. 23:4)
44. Stingeth like _____ adder. (Prov. 23:32)
46. Nickname for Isaac.
47. _____, I am with you always. (Matt. 28:20)
49. Abihail was Mordecai's _____. (Es. 2:15)
51. To blend together.
52. These things I will that thou _____ constantly. (Titus 3:8)
54. From everlasting, and to everlasting. _____. (Ps. 41:13)
55. _____ ye then be risen with Christ. (Col. 3:1)
56. Ye call me _____ and Lord. (John 13:13)
57. Abraham...died in a good old _____. (Gen. 25:8)

DOWN CLUES

1. The apostle who was a tax collector. (Matt. 10:3)
2. Abijam's son. (1 Kgs. 15:8)
3. The first month. (Es. 3:7)
4. The fishermen...were washing their _____. (Luke 5:2)
5. A fermented drink.
6. _____ found grace in the eyes of the Lord. (Gen. 6:8)
7. The _____ wise God, be honour. (1 Tim. 1:17)
8. There is a woman that hath a familiar spirit at _____ -dor. (1 Sam. 28:7)
9. David's firstborn. (2 Sam. 3:2)
10. _____ hospitality one to another. (1 Pet. 4:9)
13. Nickname for Albert.

74

17. He came unto his _____. (John 1:11)
19. A yellowish-brown color.
20. Six hundred shekels of gold went to one _____. (1 Kgs. 10:16)
22. They have _____ from the faith. (1 Tim. 6:10)
23. Suffer me that I may _____ the pillars. (Judg. 16:26)
25. The _____ of violence is in their hands. (Isa. 59:6)
27. They look and _____ upon me. (Ps. 22:17)
28. _____ up thy bed, and walk. (Matt. 9:6)
29. Thou art _____. (Acts. 12:15)

31. Children _____ your parents in the Lord. (Eph. 6:1)
33. Abda's grandfather. (Neh. 11:17)
34. There shall be as the _____ of an olive tree. (Isa. 24:13)
37. One of David's sons. (1 Chron. 3:5)
38. Shaphat's father. (1 Chron. 27:29)
41. Short for Texas.
43. A particular quality surrounding a person or thing.
45. He drew _____ to behold it. (Acts. 7:31)
48. Put _____ the old man with his deeds. (Col. 3:9)
50. Names (abbr.).
53. I am (contraction).

75

PUZZLE 37

Joan F. Watt

ACROSS CLUES

1. When thou makest a feast, call the poor, the _____. (Luke 14:13)
6. He came unto his _____. (John 1:11)
9. Exist.
10. Set thine house in _____. (2 Kgs. 20:1)
11. Beam cross section.
13. Come upon.
14. Harbor.
16. In the way wherein I walked have they privily laid a _____ for me. (Ps. 142:3)
17. Year (abbr.).
18. Fermented beverage.
20. Loafer.
22. Encountered.
24. The men of Beth-el and _____. (Ezra 2:28)
25. Turn yourselves from your _____. (Ezek. 14:6)

29. See!
30. There shall come a _____ out of Jacob. (Num. 24:17)
32. Record.
33. Short for James.
34. First female.
35. Louse eggs.
36. Recedes.
39. Short for Albert.
40. Overhead transportation.
41. Roman numeral four.
42. A Hindu queen.
43. Governing assembly.
45. Greatest of them _____ to the least. (Jonah 3:5)
46. Note in musical scale.
48. The eye cannot say unto the hand, I have no _____ of thee. (1 Cor. 12:21)
49. Fuss.
51. Direction.
52. Wherewith one may _____ another. (Rom. 14:19)

DOWN CLUES

1. Mothers.
2. Space for sports event.
3. Perfect.
4. *Meter* in London.
5. Pertaining to Celts of Scotland.
6. We ought to _____ God. (Acts 5:29)
7. Come to me, all you who are _____ and burdened. (Matt. 11:28 NIV)
8. Short rest.
11. Part of verb *to be*.
12. Person of Moab.
15. Praise him with the _____ and dance. (Ps. 150:4)
19. For I know whom I have _____. (2 Tim. 1:12)
21. He was not that Light, but was sent to bear _____. (John 1:8)
23. Laid it in his own new _____. (Matt. 27:60)
24. Equally.
26. Give us day by day our _____ bread. (Luke 11:3)
27. Choose.
28. Course of study.
31. Assist.
37. Man shall not live by _____ alone. (Matt. 4:4)
38. Girl's name.
44. But ye have made it a _____ of thieves. (Matt. 21:13)
47. His mother marvelled _____ those things which were spoken of him. (Luke 2:33)
50. Coming from.

77

PUZZLE 38

Deborah Justice

ACROSS CLUES

1. Ahiam the son of _____.
   (2 Sam. 23:33)
6. _____, whose name was
   Belteshazzar. (Dan. 2:26)
10. She bare unto Amram _____ and
    Moses, and Miriam their sister.
    (Num. 26:59)
11. Bring _____ offering, and come
    into his courts. (Ps. 96:8)
12. Glass (abbr.).
13. Compete.
14. And they following _____ helped
    him. (1 Kgs. 1:7)
18. And _____, and Gibbethon, and
    Baalath. (Josh. 19:44)
19. I bear up the pillars of it. _____.
    (Ps. 75:3)
21. Confounded be all they that serve
    graven _____. (Ps. 97:7)
23. Negative.
24. Doctor of Dental Surgery (abbr.).
26. Created.
27. Salt Lake City is the capital.
28. Not applicable.
29. Daniel, _____, Joel.
32. If the _____ be on the fleece only.
    (Judg. 6:37)
35. Associate Press (abbr.).
36. In the twinkling of _____ eye.
    (1 Cor. 15:52)
37. There came two angels to _____.
    (Gen. 19:1)
40. Samantha (nickname).
42. A little water _____ _____ vessel.
    (1 Kgs. 17:10; 2 words)
43. A tool with a sharp blade.

45. And the lot fell upon _____.
    (Acts 1:26)
49. Pointed piece of metal.
51. A period of time.
52. Tensile strength (abbr.).
53. Crown (abbr.).
54. His father saw him, and had com-
    passion, and _____. (Luke 15:20)
55. The twentieth to _____.
    (1 Chron. 24:16)

DOWN CLUES

1. And to _____ that which was lost.
   (Luke 19:10)
2. And there followed _____ and fire.
   (Rev. 8:7)
3. The governor under _____ the king.
   (2 Cor. 11:32)
4. Nickname for Rosemary.
5. A people great, and many, and tall,
   as the _____s. (Deut. 2:10)
6. Why did _____ remain in ships?
   (Judg. 5:17)
7. Of mint and _____ and cummin.
   (Matt. 23:23)
8. _____ the son of Nathan.
   (2 Sam. 23:36)
9. _____ the son of Jaareoregim.
   (2 Sam. 21:19)
15. And _____, greet you. (Col. 4:14)
16. Jamin, and _____, and Jachin.
    (Ex. 6:15)
17. God's Son.
20. Sent unto _____ king of Hebron.
    (Josh. 10:3)
22. _____, Exodus, Leviticus.
25. To let fall.
29. A hand tool used for pounding or
    driving in.
30. Opposite of west.

31. _____ the daughter of Zibeon. (Gen. 36:2)
33. Gained victory.
34. _____ the mount of Olives. (Luke 22:39)
38. A time to mourn, and a time to _____. (Ec. 3:4)
39. Northern state.
41. Til thou hast paid the very last _____. (Luke 12:59)
44. Extra large (abbr.).
46. And Pispah, and _____. 2(1 Chron. 7:38)
47. Light yellowish brown color.
48. A type of tree.
50. Prepared an _____ to the saving of his house. (Heb. 11:7)

PUZZLE 39

Janet W. Adkins

ACROSS CLUES

1. God is _____ to graff them in again. (Rom. 11:23)
5. Arrest.
8. A light that shineth in a _____ place. (2 Pet. 1:19)
12. First king of Israel.
13. The self.
14. Great lake.
15. The sons of Appaim; _____. (1 Chron. 2:31)
16. Cat's hand.
17. Aromatic spice.
18. And _____, Hanan, Anan. (Neh. 10:26)
19. Tooth covering.
21. Then Jacob gave Esau bread and pottage of _____ tiles. (Gen. 25:34)
22. Let him _____ evil. (1 Pet. 3:11)
25. Become downcast.
29. Like the roaring of the _____. (Isa. 5:30)
30. *Much _____ About Nothing.*
31. Better...a man who controls his _____ than one who takes a city. (Prov. 16:32 NIV)
35. And I will give you _____s according to mine heart. (Jer. 3:15)
37. As the loving hind and the pleasant _____. (Prov. 5:19)
38. That we may _____ mercy, and find grace. (Heb. 4:16)
41. But I say unto you that ye _____ not evil. (Matt. 5:39)
45. _____ without ceasing. (1 Thes. 5:17)
46. Belonging to the King of Bashan. (Num. 21:33)

48. _____ was _____ son of Gad. (Gen. 46:16; 2 words)
49. Ireland.
50. Court, pursue.
51. Military standing.
52. Thou art _____, O Lord. (Ps. 119:151)
53. Negative prefix.
54. Angel (French).

DOWN CLUES

1. Continent.
2. Strike with a heavy blow.
3. For by the mounting up of _____ th with weeping. (Isa. 15:5)
4. Tishbite prophet. (1 Kgs. 17:1)
5. Relation of Lot to Abraham.
6. Turkish ruler.
7. Put on... _____ of mercies. (Col. 3:12)
8. For I will _____ of thee. (Job 38:3)
9. Esrom begat _____. (Matt. 1:3)
10. Chinese staple.
11. Main stem of a ship.
20. Teacher's organization.
22. Superlative ending.
23. We shall _____ him as he is. (1 John 3:2)
24. Machine part.
26. Dative (abbr.).
27. Former name of Tokyo.
28. The ungodly shall not stand in the judgment, _____ sinners in the congregation. (Ps. 1:5)
32. And the _____ of faith shall save the sick. (Jam. 5:15)
33. Not "a" or "u."
34. Fame.
35. Who being...the express image of his _____. (Heb. 1:3)
36. _____ fled away...to the tent of Jael. (Judg. 4:17)

38. Put him to an _____ shame. (Heb. 6:6)
39. Type of cheese.
40. Fictional plantation.
42. Neighbor of Iraq.

43. Is any merry? let him _____ psalms. (Jam. 5:13)
44. Arise, and _____ up thy bed and walk. (Mark 2:9)
47. Sticky substance.

PUZZLE 40

Janet W. Adkins

ACROSS CLUES

1. He _____ for apples.
5. Little drink.
8. The sons of Merari...Zaccur and _____. (1 Chron. 24:27)
12. Great amount (2 words).
13. Belonging to a girl.
14. Thou art _____, O Lord. (Ps. 119:151)
15. And a certain centurion's servant, who was _____ unto him, was sick. (Luke 7:2)
16. Indian dress.
17. From Shepham to Riblah on the east side of _____. (Num. 34:11)
19. The voice of the Lord divideth the _____ of fire. (Ps. 29:7)
21. For there is no work, nor _____ ...in the grave. (Ec. 9:10)
24. Good time.
25. Descendant of Eri. (Num. 26:16)
26. And Ahab told _____ all that Elijah had done. (1 Kgs. 19:1)
30. By faith _____ch was translated. (Heb. 11:5)
31. Pitch.
32. Eggs.
33. To _____ such an one unto Satan. (1 Cor. 5:5)
36. Accepted belief.
38. Teacher's organization.
39. Harsh.
40. Sought how they might take him by _____, and put him to death. (Mark 14:1)
43. Pod vegetable.
44. _____ avis: rarity.
45. Bringing gold and silver, ivory, and _____(s). (1 Kgs. 10:22)
47. Calendar entry.
51. What the little engine said (2 words).
52. Pasture.
53. And the Lord God planted a garden eastward in _____. (Gen. 2:8)
54. As the twig is _____, so grows the branch.
55. Noah entered the _____. (Gen. 7:7)
56. Foolish man built his house upon the _____. (Matt. 7:26)

DOWN CLUES

1. Cast the _____ away. (Matt. 13:48)
2. Bullfight cheer.
3. Feather scarf.
4. I am in a _____ betwixt two. (Phil. 1:23)
5. Let your light so _____ before men. (Matt. 5:16)
6. That is (Latin).
7. To offer for acceptance.
8. Mad.
9. First cast out the _____ out of thine own eye. (Matt. 7:5)
10. It is a _____ thing that the king requireth. (Dan. 2:11)
11. Spring flower.
18. Frozen water.
20. Bethel...was called _____ at the first. (Gen. 28:19)
21. Let us love...in _____ and in truth. (1 John 3:18)
22. Sea eagle.
23. String instrument.
26. Glass container.
27. This is now _____ of my bones. (Gen. 2:23)

28. So shall we _____ be with the Lord. (1 Thes. 4:17)
29. Not early.
31. Beverage.
34. There shall be no more thence an _____ of days. (Isa. 65:20)
35. Former serviceman/woman.
36. Golf peg.
37. Avoids.
39. Be swift to hear, slow to _____. (Jam. 1:19)
40. Away in a manger, no _____ for a bed.

41. And rejoiceth as a strong man to run a _____. (Ps. 19:5)
42. The children of Dishan...Uz, and _____. (Gen. 36:28)
45. In this manner.
46. Each.
48. Modern form of name of Lamech's wife. (Gen. 4:19)
49. _____ virgins; _____ lepers.
50. He that endureth to the _____ shall be saved. (Matt. 10:22)

PUZZLE 41

Janet W. Adkins

ACROSS CLUES

1. Tennis name Steffi _____.
5. Because their _____ is come unto me. (1 Sam. 9:16)
8. A Christmas carol.
12. Volcanic output.
13. Aaron and _____ stayed up his hands. (Ex. 17:12)
14. The people that followed _____ prevailed. (1 Kgs. 16:22)
15. City of Judah. (Josh. 15:32,50)
16. Sounds of questioning.
17. Blood vessel.
18. Practicer of divination.
20. From then until now.
21. The ungodly shall not stand in the judgment, _____ sinners in the congregation. (Ps. 1:5)
22. Facial twitch.
23. I counsel thee to buy of me gold tried in the _____. (Rev. 3:18)
26. Spake of his _____ which he should accomplish at Jerusalem. (Luke 9:31)
30. Blackbird.
31. Thieves _____ through and steal. (Matt. 6:19)
33. But I will not with ink and _____ write unto thee. (3 John 13)
34. Tambourines. (1 Sam. 18:6)
36. Went rapidly.
37. Compass direction.
38. Stadium cheer.
40. Sought how they might take him by _____. (Mark 14:1)
43. Taking away.
47. _____rn unto me, and I will return unto you. (Mal. 3:7)
48. Hawaiian dish.
49. Ye who sometimes _____ far off are made nigh. (Eph. 2:13)
50. Belonging to the mother of Hezekiah. (2 Kgs. 18:1,2)
51. The _____ shall not smite thee by day. (Ps. 121:6)
52. Sicilian volcano.
53. Stand open.
54. Possessive pronoun.
55. I am not worthy that thou shouldest enter under my _____. (Luke 7:6)

DOWN CLUES

1. A wise son maketh a _____ father. (Prov. 10:1)
2. Indian princess.
3. Tel _____.
4. There arose a mighty _____ in that land. (Luke 15:14)
5. Shall _____ up his wife which he hath taken. (Deut. 24:5)
6. German river.
7. Years. (abbr.).
8. New at an activity.
9. A sign of the future.
10. Norse explorer.
11. Thou shalt bind this _____ of scarlet thread in the window. (Josh 2:18)
19. Negative reply.
20. I was _____, and ye visited me. (Matt. 25:36)
22. Beverage.
23. All the _____ is the Lord's. (Lev. 3:16)
24. _____ _____ moment, in the twinkling of an eye. (1 Cor. 15:52; 2 words)
25. And the _____, which the Lord God had taken from man. (Gen. 2:22)

26. Desert (abbr.).
27. Appendix (abbr.).
28. Blessed are the pure in heart: for they shall _____ God. (Matt. 5:8)
29. From the beginning of the year even unto the _____ of the year. (Deut. 11:12)
31. Bring forth the _____ robe. (Luke 15:22)
32. Route (abbr.).
35. This evil people, which _____ to hear my words. (Jer. 13:10)
36. Light rain.
38. For the righteous God trieth the hearts and _____. (Ps. 7:9)
39. I _____ Alpha and Omega. (Rev. 1:8)
40. Jagged cliff.
41. And they slew the kings of Midian...Zur...Hur, and _____. (Num. 31:8)
42. Toppling over.
43. Drive out.
44. Turn down.
45. River in Italy.
46. His _____ also shall not wither. (Ps. 1:3)
48. Greek letter.

PUZZLE 42

Janet W. Adkins

ACROSS CLUES

1. Brought him to an _____.
   (Luke 10:34)
4. The house was filled with the _____
   of the ointment. (John 12:3,
   Am. spelling)
8. Clip.
12. Deliver thyself as a _____ from the
    hunter. (Prov. 6:5)
13. This is now _____ of my bones.
    (Gen. 2:23)
14. Greek letter.
15. Of birds (prefix).
16. Very (French).
17. Went by plane.
18. Lunatic.
19. Again he _____ the same sacri-
    fices. (Heb. 10:11 NIV)
21. Iowa (abbr.).
22. Rhode Island (abbr.).
23. We remember the leeks, and the
    _____. (Num. 11:5)
26. Leah was _____ eyed. (Gen. 29:17)
30. Teachers' organization.
31. And Bezaleel the son of _____.
    (Ex. 38:22)
32. God shall send them _____
    delusion. (2 Thes. 2:11)
35. And John bare _____, saying, I saw
    the Spirit. (John 1:32)
37. Each (abbr.).
38. And she [Shuah] conceived, and
    bore a son; and he called his name
    _____. (Gen. 38:3)
39. I will not be an _____. (Isa. 3:7)
43. The disciples asked him again of
    the same _____. (Mark 10:10)

47. Naum, which was the son of _____.
    (Luke 3:25)
48. God (Spanish).
50. Then enquired he of them the hour
    be began to _____nd. (John 4:52)
51. The blind receive their sight, and
    the _____ walk. (Matt. 11:5)
52. Between (combining form).
53. 1/1000 inch.
54. Plutonium, arsenic (chem.
    symbols).
55. Scottish denials.
56. Isle in England.

DOWN CLUES

1. A duke of Edom. (Gen. 36:43)
2. Suddenly bright star.
3. No (German).
4. For whoso findeth me...shall
   _____ favour of the Lord.
   (Prov. 8:35)
5. Also called Tabitha. (Acts 9:36)
6. First number.
7. My strong habitation whereunto I
   may continually _____. (Ps. 71:3)
8. Spat.
9. Part in a play.
10. To do again and again: _____ate.
11. They shall give unto the priest the
    shoulder...and the _____(pl.).
    (Deut. 18:3)
20. Response of disgust (archaic).
23. Belonging to a son of Peleth.
    (Num. 16:1)
24. Let his _____ that he hath hid catch
    himself. (Ps. 35:8)
25. Adjective suffix.
27. A pair.
28. If any of you do _____ from the
    truth. (Jam. 5:19)
29. I will _____ evil beasts out of the
    land. (Lev. 26:6)

33. Born.
34. The Lord God planted a _____ eastward in Eden. (Gen. 2:8)
35. Distant.
36. Deletes.
39. My _____ cometh from the Lord. (Ps. 121:2)
40. Jacob's twin.
41. Woman's name.

42. Or if he finds lost property and _____ about it. (Lev. 6:3 NIV)
44. But the tongue can no man _____. (Jam. 3:8)
45. Man's name.
46. Because thou didst _____ on the Lord. (2 Chron 16:8)
49. For I am _____ _____ strait betwixt two. (Phil. 1:23; 2 words)

PUZZLE 43

Janet W. Adkins

ACROSS CLUES

1. And _____ things of the world ...hath God chosen. (1 Cor. 1:28)
5. He maketh me to _____ down in green pastures. (Ps. 23:2)
8. Redecorate.
12. Swiss mountains.
13. Intent.
14. Of _____ the family of the Arodites. (Num. 26:17)
15. To drive out.
16. Compete.
17. Nathaniel to his friends.
18. Scold severely.
20. King Solomon made a navy of ships...on the shore of the _____ _____. (1 Kgs. 9:26; 2 words)
22. Pitch.
23. Spanish *gold*.
24. She called his name _____: because I drew him out of the water. (Ex. 2:10)
27. As an _____ harder than flint have I made thy forehead. (Ezek. 3:9)
30. Rhode Island (abbr.).
31. Elevated trains.
32. Yes (Spanish).
33. I will incline mine ear to a _____ (Ps. 49:4)
36. A _____ of David.
38. National Rifle Association.
39. A son of God. (Gen. 46:16)
40. Who gave himself a _____ for all. (1 Tim. 2:6)
43. And the sons of Eliab; _____, and Dathan. (Num. 26:9)
47. Sufficient (archaic).
48. Money earned on account (abbr.).

50. _____torian: Roman bodyguard.
51. British princess.
52. Golf peg.
53. If a man die, shall he _____ again? (Job 14:14)
54. The young lions _____ after their prey. (Ps. 104:21)
55. First the blade, then the _____. (Mark 4:28)
56. Crisis: _____rgency.

DOWN CLUES

1. A cutting remark.
2. Medicinal plant.
3. Prod.
4. That he might know your _____, and comfort your hearts. (Col. 4:8)
5. Thou shalt also make a _____ of brass. (Ex. 30:18)
6. Roman numeral 3.
7. The hand of the Lord... smote them with _____. (1 Sam. 5:6)
8. Chosen in no specific pattern.
9. Historical periods.
10. A sword is upon the liars; and they shall _____. (Jer. 50:36)
11. Greek auditoriums.
19. British farewells.
21. Equal Rights Amendment.
25. Mouth.
26. _____, we would see Jesus. (John 12:21)
27. Pub drink.
28. _____ did that which was right in the eyes of the Lord. (1 Kgs. 15:11)
29. Nothing.
31. Inhabitnt of Elam.
34. A soft _____ turneth away wrath. (Prov. 15:1)
35. Sibling.
36. Earlier (prefix).

37. The _____ believeth every word. (Prov. 14:15)
39. He cannot _____ into the kingdom of God. (John 3:5)
40. Backward part.
41. _____ Domini.

42. Nickname for Wynona.
44. There stood up a priest with _____ and with Thummim. (Ezra 2:63)
45. Overhanging roof edge.
46. Southern Gen.: R.E._____.
49. Teachers' organization (abbr.).

PUZZLE 44

Glenn G. Luscher

ACROSS CLUES

1. A cake. (Ex. 16:31)
3. Mountain sheep. (Deut. 14:5)
8. A skiff.
9. A snake. (Ps. 140:3)
13. Trinitrotoluene (abbr.).
14. Portable steps.
16. An evening meal.
17. Perpetual. (Rom. 1:20)
19. Son of Zebulun. (Gen. 46:14)
20. Greek word signifying "the last." (Rev. 1:8)
22. Son of Appaim. (1 Chron. 2:31)
24. New Testament (abbr.).
26. Feminine case pronoun.
29. Builder of Nineveh. (Gen. 10:11)
31. Of the flesh. (Rom. 8:7)
32. Another name for father.
33. Truck driver's vehicle.
34. Not heavy.
35. Alternating current (abbr.).
36. Mexican painter Jose Clemente

_____.

39. A promise. (Luke 1:73)
40. Same as tea cart.
44. Masculine pronoun.
45. Northwest Territory (abbr.).
46. Small ones.
47. Secret Service (abbr.).

DOWN CLUES

1. Sea monsters. (Gen. 1:21)
2. Food for animals.
3. Collapsible bed.
4. Used for gripping.
5. What you put on. (Prov. 7:10)
6. A furnace. (Ps. 21:9)
7. A net. (2 Tim. 2:26)
10. Fruit of the palm.
11. Where Og fought a battle. (Num. 21:33)
12. Cuts out. (Hosea 13:8)
15. Symbol for radium.
18. The grandmother of Timothy. (2 Tim. 1:5)
21. Those who are greedy eaters.
23. To set apart. (Ex. 40:9)
25. Gives instruction.
26. A book or roll. (Rev. 6:14)
27. John was clothed with camel's _____. (Mark 1:6)
28. Used to make alkaloids.
30. To hang loosely.
32. All her _____ are peace. (Prov. 3:17)
37. Buddhist sect developed in India.
38. A feline.
41. A preposition.
42. To move or proceed.
43. Old Testament (abbr.).

PUZZLE 45

Deborah Justice

ACROSS CLUES

1. _____, come forth, and flee. (Zech. 2:6)
3. _____, a prophetess. (Luke 2:36)
6. But a faithful man who can _____? (Prov. 20:6)
10. Alpha and _____. (Rev. 1:8)
12. To put into action.
14. Jacob's brother. (Gen. 27:6)
15. Bath-sheba's first husband. (2 Sam. 11:3)
16. Make thee _____ ark. (Gen. 6:14)
17. To make a mistake.
18. Spanish for *Yes.*
19. And the Lord shall _____ thee. (Is. 58:11)
20. Male parent (plural).
22. Short for Timothy.
23. And he went out to meet _____. (2 Chron. 15:2)
24. In no way.
25. A son of Benjamin. (Gen. 46:21)
26. _____ vera lotion.

28. A family's dwelling place.
29. Book between Jonah and Nahum (abbr.).
30. Missionary kid (abbr.).
31. Ex officio (abbr.).
32. For the Lord God is a _____. (Ps. 84:11)
34. This _____ that.
36. Not applicable (abbr.).
37. And love unto all the _____. (Eph. 1:15)
40. A brief sleep.
41. _____ ye therefore, and teach. (Matt. 28:19)
42. The howling thereof unto _____. (Isa. 15:8)
43. Come into the land of _____. (Lev. 14:34)
46. Jump on one foot.
47. No report (abbr.).
48. To express in words.
49. Opposite of 46 Down.
50. Strive to _____ in. (Luke 13:24)

DOWN CLUES

1. In my Father's _____. (John 14:2)
2. _____ to reign over Israel. (1 Kgs. 16:23)
3. Haman the _____(s). (Es. 8:3)
4. Jonah, Micah, _____.
5. And Dimonah, and _____. (Josh. 15:22)
6. _____ my sheep. (John 21:16)
7. That is to be ruler in _____. (Micah 5:2)
8. Box of ointment of spike_____. (Mark 14:3)
9. Dutch (abbr.).
13. For my son _____. (Philemon 10).
21. It is time to _____ the Lord. (Hosea 10:12)
22. Thomas (nickname).
24. Midday.
25. Joshaviah, the sons of _____. (1 Chron. 11:46)
26. Movement.
27. To leave out.
28. Thus the _____ and the earth were finished. (Gen. 2:1)
33. Shemiramoth, and Jehiel, and _____. (1 Chron. 15:20)
35. Postpone.
38. Greek word meaning "love."
39. Thou art my _____. (Heb. 1:5)
43. A prefix meaning "jointly."
44. Go to the _____, thou sluggard. (Prov. 6:6)
45. We _____ going to attend church on Sunday.
46. _____ brought me up also out of a horrible pit. (Ps. 40:2)

PUZZLE 46

Glenn G. Luscher

ACROSS CLUES

1. Day of rest.
4. Adam was the first.
6. Southwest (abbr.).
7. Another name for Mother.
8. Stand fast in _____ spirit. (Phil. 1:27)
10. The strength of an _____. (Num. 23:22)
13. Nighttime movie.
15. A sleeping noise.
16. Saul's father. (1 Sam. 10:21)
18. Used for hearing.
20. Built rugged.
22. The _____ of wisdom is above rubies. (Job 27:18)
24. It _____ upon each of them. (Acts 2:3)
26. Automobile.
27. Cooling device.
28. Abraham's original name. (Gen. 17:5)
31. What rabbits do.

94

33. Uninvited picnic guest.
34. _____ the Arbite. (2 Sam. 23:35)
35. Another name for Father.
36. Road (abbr.).
38. Province of Asia Minor. (Acts 16:7)
40. With your _____ girded. (Ex. 12:11)
41. Frozen water.
43. Container used for cooking.
45. Move quickly.
46. Mary's sister. (Luke 10:38, 39)
47. A preposition.

DOWN CLUES

1. Peanut coverings.
2. Native of Tekoa. (Amos 1:1)
3. Tale or heavy thread.
4. Another name I call myself.
5. A conjunction.
6. Galilee is one.
9. Name of a Simeonite captain.
   (1 Chron. 4:42)
11. Without delay.
12. Lamech's son. (Gen. 5:28,29)
13. Extending far downward.
14. Unable to speak.
17. Exceedingly warm.
19. A bowlike curved line.
21. A city of Benjamin. (Josh. 21:17)
23. Collected agricultural product.
24. Name of Orphan Annie's dog.
25. Opposite of near.
27. One who raises livestock.
28. Son of Nadab. (1 Chron. 2:30)
29. One who speaks to cause injury.
    (1 Cor. 5:11)
30. A miry place. (Ezek. 47:11)
32. A mother or father.
37. A snake. (Job 20:16)
39. Male offspring.
42. California (abbr.).
44. Alcoholics Anonymous (abbr.).

PUZZLE 47

Debra Michaels

ACROSS CLUES

1. Birthplace of our Lord. (Matt. 2:1)
9. Ye know how that a good while _____. (Acts 15:7)
12. Maternal grandfather of King Josiah. (2 Kgs. 22:1)
13. Gamaliel, a _____ of the law. (Acts 5:34)
14. Original home of Abraham's family. (Gen. 11:28)
16. Kilogram (abbr.).
18. City destroyed by fire from heaven. (Gen. 19:24)
20. Her clothing is _____ and purple. (Prov. 31:22)
22. Let _____ esteem others better than themselves. (Phil. 2:3)
24. A plain in Babylon. (Dan. 3:1)
26. Cain asked, _____ I my brother's keeper? (Gen. 4:9)
27. Prepare a table for that _____. (Isa. 65:11)
28. Was in prison with Paul at Philippi. (Acts 16:25)
30. The lot is cast into the _____. (Prov. 16:33)
31. The Lord _____ is my strength. (Isa. 12:2)
33. God, who is _____ in mercy. (Eph. 2:4)
34. To wound with the teeth.
36. Two-wheeled vehicle used for travel and war. (Gen. 41:43)
39. Prefix meaning *in*.
40. Son of David. (2 Sam. 5:13-15)
44. Singular of the verb *have*.
46. Symbol for the chemical element barium.
48. Elder brother of Moses and Miriam. (Num. 26:59)
49. King of Bashan. (Num. 21:33)
50. Twig broom for sweeping. (Isa. 14:23)
53. Symbol for the chemical element chlorine.
54. Long period of time.
55. A sleeveless linen garment worn by priests. (Ex. 28:4)
56. Yard (abbr.).

DOWN CLUES

1. Disciples let Saul down by the wall in a _____. (Acts 9:25)
2. Nickname for Edward.
3. To make lace.
4. Greeting.
5. Los Angeles (abbr.).
6. Son of Bilhan. (1 Chron. 7:10)
7. Children of Gad called the altar _____, meaning witness. (Josh. 22:34)
8. A bushy head of hair.
9. The time is _____ hand. (Rev. 1:3)
10. Hungarian stew.
11. Oregon (abbr.).
15. Thy _____ and thy staff comfort me. (Ps. 23:4)
17. Bulb with a strong smell.
18. Atroth, _____, and Jaazer. (Num. 32:35)
19. Descendant of Mushi. (Num. 3:33)
20. Healing ointment.
21. Kilometer (abbr.).
23. Trainers in athletics.
25. To disturb the peace.
29. Alcoholics Anonymous.
32. Black.
35. Job's country. (Job 1:1)
37. Leniency shown to a guilty person.
38. Footwear.

41. Pennsylvania (abbr.).
42. Exclamation of derision.
43. How is the _____ become dim!
    (Lam. 4:1)
45. Past.

46. Insect.
47. Hooded venomous serpent.
    (Rom. 3:13)
51. Ohio (abbr.).
52. Missouri (abbr.).

PUZZLE 48

Janice A. Buhl

ACROSS CLUES

1. Moses stretched forth his hand over the _____. (Ex 14:27)
4. _____, a lamb stood on the mount Sion. (Rev. 14:1)
7. _____, holy, holy, Lord God Almighty. (Rev. 4:8)
10. Do they not _____ that devise evil? (Prov. 14:22)
11. I will bring thee unto _____ place. (Num. 23:27)
14. Ye shall not _____ the Lord. (Deut. 6:16)
16. The _____ out of the wood doth waste it. (Ps. 80:13)
17. Israel sighed by _____ of the bond age. (Ex. 2:23)
19. Give _____ unto the law. (Isa. 1:10)
21. Or a bright spot, white, and some what _____. (Lev. 13:19)
23. Children, _____ your parents. (Eph. 6:1)
25. Judah took a wife for _____ his firstborn. (Gen. 38:6)
26. Wound with a pointed weapon.
28. Fourth note in the musical scale.
29. _____, so would we have it. (Ps. 35:25)
30. He sent and signified it _____ his angel. (Rev. 1:1)
31. Do, Re, Mi, _____.
32. He turned and went away in a _____. (2 Kgs. 5:12)
35. Yet _____ they eat the passover. (2 Chron. 30:18)
37. And the man said unto _____, I am he. (1 Sam. 4:16)
39. Louisiana (abbr.).
40. _____ let not the Lord be angry. (Gen. 18:30)
42. If any man shall _____ unto these things. (Rev. 22:18)
44. The glory of the Lord shone round _____. (Luke 2:9)

47. And _____ came to pass. (Amos 7:2)
49. The best of them is as a _____. (Micah 7:4)
51. The scribes and the Pharisees began to _____ him vehemently. (Luke 11:53)
52. The book of the vision of _____ the Elkoshite. (Nahum 1:1)
54. Balaam the son of ___. (Micah 6:5)
56. Suffix meaning "to make" or "to become."
57. Strain at a _____, and swallow a camel. (Matt. 23:24)
58. Shall _____ away ungodliness from Jacob. (Rom 11:26)

DOWN CLUES

1. She bore a son, and called his name _____. (Gen. 4:25)
2. Sir, come down _____ my child die. (John 4:49)
3. _____ yourselves likewise with the same mind. (1 Pet. 4:1)
4. It is vain for you to rise up early, to sit up _____. (Ps. 127:2)
5. _____ the morrow they left the horsemen to go with him. (Acts 23:32)
6. So I _____ upon him, and slew him. (2 Sam. 1:10)
7. Then she arose with _____ daughters in law. (Ruth 1:6)
8. He struck it into the pan, _____ kettle. (1 Sam. 2:14)
9. In the second _____ of Darius. (Zech. 1:7)
12. And ye shall _____ the feast of unleavened bread. (Ex. 12:17)
13. Christ sitteth on the right _____ of God. (Col. 3:1)
15. O Lord God of hosts, hear my _____. (Ps. 84:8)
18. Into your hand _____ they delivered. (Gen. 9:2)
19. Established (abbr.).

20. _____ the son of Kolaiah. (Jer. 29:21)
22. Lord, that thou shalt call me _____. (Hosea 2:16)
23. I will offer it up for a burnt _____. (Judg. 11:31)
24. For he served _____, and worshipped him. (1 Kgs. 22:53)
27. Short for *good-bye*.
29. Anno Domini (abbr.).
33. I will cause an _____ of war to be heard. (Jer. 49:2)
34. Menahem the son of _____. (2 Kgs. 15:14)
36. Sarah heard it in the tent _____. (Gen. 18:10)
38. He did evil _____ the sight of the Lord. (1 Kgs. 22:52)

41. Were not the Ethiopians and the Lubims a _____ host? (2 Chron. 16:8)
43. I forgave thee all that _____. (Matt. 18:32)
45. Let them not fail to _____ the fat. (1 Sam. 2:16)
46. Sisera fled away on his feet to the _____. (Judg. 4:17)
48. Preserve hides.
49. _____ Jesus beheld them. (Matt. 19:26)
50. And _____ lived two and thirty years. (Gen. 11:20)
53. He saith among the trumpets, _____, ha. (Job. 39:25)
55. Who hath ascended up into heaven, _____ descended? (Prov.30:4)

PUZZLE 49

Mrs. Chester Vance Jr.

ACROSS CLUES

1. _____ I pray you. (Gen. 37:6)
4. King of _____, and Tidal. (Gen. 14:1)
7. _____ shall judge. (Gen. 49:16)
10. _____ of the Chaldees. (Gen. 15:7)
11. The king of _____. (Gen. 40:5)
12. Plane surface having bounds.
13. Alcoholics Anonymous (abbr.).
14. _____ light.
15. Who shall _____ thee. (Gen. 49:25)
17. A _____ of money. (Ex. 21:30)
19. _____, and Naphtali. (Ex. 1:4)
20. The hole of the _____. (Isa. 11:8)
21. Prepaid (abbr.).
24. Intensive care.
26. _____ of the house. (Gen. 43:19)
27. My _____ shall not go down. (Gen. 42:38)
29. Called their name _____. (Gen. 5:2)
32. Oklahoma (abbr.).
34. Red Cross (abbr.).
35. Gone six _____. (2 Sam. 6:13)
37. _____ wept. (Gen. 50:17)
39. Chief male character in story.
40. On top of.
41. _____ sinful nation. (Isa. 1:4)
42. Nickname of Deborah.
44. Skin or husk of grain.
46. Roman numeral for fifty.
47. East Indies (abbr.).
48. There was _____ water in it. (Gen. 37:24)
49. Poti-pherah, priest of _____. (Gen. 41:45)
51. But _____ Joseph's brother. (Gen. 42:4)
55. What he sayeth to you, _____. (Gen. 41:55)
56. English (abbr.).
57. These _____ words. (Gen. 44:6)

DOWN CLUES

1. _____ the Archite. (2 Sam. 15:32)
2. Descendant of Judah. (1 Chron. 4:21)
3. They do _____. (Ruth 2:9)
4. _____ were dim. (Gen. 27:1)
5. Low pressure.
6. Music term.
7. What will become of his _____. (Gen. 37:20)
8. Thousands and thousands of years (Eng. spelling).
9. Girl's name.
12. _____ it shall come to pass. (1 Sam. 2:36)
13. Swiss mountain.
16. The servant which is _____ from his master. (Deut. 23:15)
18. Put sackcloth _____ his loins. (Gen. 37:34)
22. Sink or drop down.
23. Measure equal to 1/12 of a foot.
25. Joseph's father. (Gen. 46:19)
28. Child that has lost his parents.
30. _____ stir him up. (Job. 41:10)
31. Dealt ye so ill with _____. (Gen. 43:6)
33. Kansas.
36. Judah spake unto him, _____, . . . (Gen. 43:3)
37. Patience of _____. (Jam. 5:11)
38. Give _____ to his commandments. (Ex. 15:26)
43. Place where his tent had _____. (Gen. 13:3)

44. _____ of the water. (Josh. 3:15)
45. There is _____ that can interpret it. (Gen. 41:15)
46. Ono, and _____. (1 Chron. 8:12)
50. Thy son's coat or _____. (Gen. 37:32)
51. Upon me _____ thy curse. (Gen. 27:13)
52. _____ one of us. (Gen. 3:22)
53. _____ and Pa.
54. Northeast.

PUZZLE 50

Mrs. Chester Vance Jr.

ACROSS CLUES

1. God of my master _____.
   (Gen. 24:42)
6. Thine only son _____. (Gen. 22:2)
10. Suffix indicating names in
    zoology.
12. Obstetrician (abbr.).
13. Idle chatter.
15. Even the men of _____. (Gen. 19:4)
17. Lifted up his _____. (Gen. 22:4)
19. Abbreviation for Micah.
20. Military cap.
23. Small deer.
25. Departed out of _____. (Gen. 12:4)
26. Vitamin _____.
27. Symbol for hydrogen.
28. Children by _____. (Gen. 16:2)
30. Lemon _____.
31. _____ the father of Lecah.
    (1 Chron. 4:21)
32. A spider: _____chnid.
33. Roman numeral for 201.

35. Pursued them unto _____. (Gen. 14:14)
37. Government issued.
39. Abram removed _____ tents. (Gen. 13:18)
40. Neither _____ thou any thing. (Gen. 22:12)
41. But _____ shall her name be. (Gen. 17:15)
43. Son of Haran. (Gen. 11:27)
44. Behind him a _____. (Gen. 22:13)
45. All that he _____. (Gen. 13:1)
47. Called the altar _____. (Josh. 22:34)
49. That I _____ bury my dead. (Gen. 23:4)
50. King of Salem. (Gen. 14:18)

DOWN CLUES

1. _____ of the Lord. (Gen. 22:15)
2. Abraham's daughter-in-law. (Gen. 24:67)
3. And Ishmael _____ son. (Gen. 17:25)
4. Bustle, fuss.
5. Assembled or created.
7. _____ shall thy seed be. (Gen. 15:5)

8. _____ and Phichol. (Gen. 21:22)
9. When he was _____. (Gen. 17:24)
11. *Ex officio.*
14. Expresses surprise or distress (Span.).
16. Get thee into the land of _____. (Gen. 22:2)
18. Dry, withered.
21. Dwelt in the wilderness of _____. (Gen. 21:21)
22. _____ the choice. (Gen. 23:6)
24. Twenty years _____. (Gen. 23:1)
27. _____ of Abram's cattle. (Gen. 13:7)
29. Sarai's handmaid. (Gen. 16:1)
34. Roman numeral for 101.
36. To make amends.
38. Abbreviation for Individual Retirement Account.
42. Behold, here I _____. (Gen. 22:1)
45. I _____ rather be a doorkeeper. (Ps. 84:10)
46. Yes (nautical).
48. Roman numeral for 600.
49. I

ANSWERS

PUZZLE 1

F	O	R		H	E	A	L		S	P	A	S
A	R	E		I	N	T	O		E	A	S	T
T	E	M	P	L	E		O	W	E		H	I
		A	I	L		U	S	E		R	A	N
S	L	I	T		O	N	E		L	O	N	G
H	I	N		F	I	G		B	E	D		
Y	E		A	L	L	O	W	E	D		R	A
		C	R	Y		D	I	G		B	E	L
W	H	A	T		A	L	T		T	A	I	L
H	E	N		A	N	Y		H	O	T		
E	A		A	W	N		R	O	O	T	E	D
A	V	E	N		A	T	E	R		L	A	Y
T	E	S	T		S	O	D	I		E	R	E

PUZZLE 2

E	D	E	N		R	O	A	M		A	G	E
	E	V	E	N	I	N	G		A	D	A	M
E	V	E			P	E	E	L		D	R	
D	I	R		O		S	O	D		D	O	
I	S	L	A	N	D	S		W	I	D	E	N
C	E	A	S	E		E	L		D	O	N	E
T		S	P		T	R	E	E		C		
	O	T		O	R	P	A	H		K	I	N
C	A	I	N		Y	E		U	S		D	O
U	R	N		R		N	U	D	E		O	R
R		G	R	E	A	T			A	I	L	
S	O		A	C	T		N	A	T	O		I
E	N	V	Y		E	A	C	H		N	O	T

PUZZLE 3

T	E	N		L	O	S	T		L	A	C	Y
R	A	I	S	I	N		O		F	O	E	
U	R	N		N	E	W		C	O	I	N	S
E	S	E		E	W	E		L	U	R	E	
		T	I		A	D	M	I	R	E		G
M	A	Y	D	A	Y		I	N	S		D	O
A	N	N	E			U	R	G	E	S		O
	D	I	N	A	H		E		L	E	A	D
W	E	N	T		O		D	O	V	E		
	S	E	I	Z	E	D		M	E	D	I	C
S			T	O		A	G	E	S		C	A
O	H		Y	O	U	R		G		Y	E	T
N	E	T			S	T	R	A	Y	E	D	

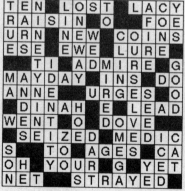

PUZZLE 4

W	I	C	K	E	D		K	O	A		N	T
I			D	E	L	I	G	H	T		O	
T	H	E	N		C	A	T		I		M	B
H	Y	P	O	C	R	I	T	E	S			B
	S	H		P	E	R	I	S	H		A	S
	S	O	W		E		M	A	A	T	H	
S	O	D	I		S	W		U	R	I	A	H
U	P		N	O		A	I		M	R		
F		A	D		Y		L	A	B	A	N	
F	A	V	O	U	R		M	O	R	E	H	
E		O	W	N		F	A	V	O	R		A
R	E	I			N	A	K	E	D		U	S
	D				R	E	D		A	R	K	

PUZZLE 5

```
WAGES   THOSE
ARISE   HELON
AT LEESAND SO
BE EKRONA AIN
IRAA SUM EDGE
ASIDE LEGIONS
  LIAR NOTA
ISETTHE AHNOT
METE ODE EDAR
NIH ADAMOR TI
AR ATAROTH HP
 BEGAT TEARS
 ERETO ENDDO
```

PUZZLE 6

```
MOSES PAUL GO
INN OVER AMEN
NEON ERECTED
D WEANS HE ER
 A V IOTA TRI
 DOE SNARE S
A TRIO RIDE E
BAH MN SOIL N
BEES BUTTER
AIR TRUSS MAT
  FEEL DEMO
EGLON BANANAS
EARTH MONTHS
```

PUZZLE 7

```
KING COME   FA
ELI HURI TB S
EAT APES HUSK
PIRAM BEFORE
 ER S ROUND
ST OAK YE IF
TOES IT SEAT
ROLE PAN VAIN
ILL B ZERO
P ABEL ANON
STAR BEND N W
 ANT E O A
END ODE KINDS
```

PUZZLE 8

```
DOTE CRUSE ME
APE POUR VEAL
LED ERS BOOK
IN YOKEFELLOW
  HENS VI E
H AS RA EACH
INSTATER NO
SOHE OAT B ND
 MURM S BETTE
 EPD OERSEER
INHAB NEAT NM
S AYER RT ETA
ME SORRY AX L
```

PUZZLE 9

```
JOB ANGEL GOD
ERE NO TO A O
SET NAZARETH
U H AHA DREAM
SHEM C R I
 ELAH HAM LS
G LIZABETH A
ASHEN RE REAL
BEE TAIL URGE
RAMS DA TERM
IT JOSEPH E
E BIO RA NEO
LO SYRIAN ASK
```

PUZZLE 10

```
MOUNTAIN LOVE
ABS NT LO OX
JESUS CARPIC
EL LAMP EDUCE
SURE ORAL REL
TSE PRO PG L
Y SCRIPTURE E
 E LEAH POD N
PREACHER M LT
OR I CHRIST
W GLORY ASIDE
EGO U DIET Y
ROD S SINS WE
```

PUZZLE 11

```
M Y S T E R Y . . . E L I
. O . D E E R . L V . N .
Z U P H . N . . C A I N .
. N O . . T W A . B L O T
. G O L D . O S L O . B .
H E R O . . R A . R I L .
O R . B A C K S L I D E R
S . C . S H E . . N O M E
P R O P H E T S . G L A D
I A M . . A H A B . . N .
T I E . O P . V A I N . W
A S S . R E V E R T . C O
L E T T E R . D E S E R T
```

PUZZLE 12

```
. L A I D . L U K E . . .
. O F F A . E S E K . . .
G I R L . N O T . P E R M
L A D Y . G A T . T R E E
A T . . E R E . . . . A T
D E B T O R . R E T I R E
. A I N . . . . . N E R .
A B D E E L . A D A I A H
B E . A B I . . . . . H E
E L O I . Y E A . A H E R
L A M B . I L L . B E N D
. E R A N . A B D I . . .
. R I N G . Y E A R . . .
```

PUZZLE 13

```
W O E . S E W . P A I . .
H U L . T O E . A B L E .
O R I G I N . A R E . D O
. E A R . P I T . D E N .
R E L Y . P A R . L I N E
I V . T I N . R A N . . .
P E R S O N . R E D E E M
. O A T . Y O U . . Y E .
E A S Y . R E D . A M E N
E R E . L O T . L I E . .
L A . C O W . B A L A A M
. M O R N . T E N . T H E
. R Y E . O D D . S I T .
```

PUZZLE 14

```
F O E . H I M . I B R I .
R U N . H O L Y . N E E D
O R D A I N E R . V A S E
. U R G E . E V E N T S .
S A R A H . T W I N . . .
A N I M . R O A S T E T H
T O N . G E N R E . N E E
E N G R A V E D . S T A R
. E V E R . T H E R E . .
G R A V E N . S O U R . .
R O S E . G E N E T I C S
I D E A . E R A S . N O E
M E A L . D I G . G O T .
```

PUZZLE 15

```
M A N A S S E H . B . B .
A P A C E . R E C E I V E
K A R T A N . B O A T . .
E R R . A . R A T E . E .
. T O . M . E L . T . M .
. W A R E . W . S H E M .
. N E S T . H O . A . . .
A N D . D . C A N A A N .
B E E . S E E . N . D . U
R E E L E D . J O N A . E
A D R I A . M . C A M E L
M E S S . E . H I S S . .
. D . T I M N A . L . . .
```

PUZZLE 16

```
F I R S T B O R N . O G .
L A I N . H I . P R A Y .
A M B A S S A D O R . Z E
M . R . A D D . I G A L .
E D G E . M . L I D . L .
S O . L U K E . E . L O .
. . . E . C . . S O W . .
I S R A E L . G O . A T .
S A U L . G . N . I . . .
A M I S S . A B S A L O M
I . N O . O D O U R . B E
A H . A D A M . E N . . .
H A G . W R I T E . B Y .
```

106

PUZZLE 17

L	O	S	T		N	E	T	S		P	V	T
E	A	S	E		O	D	E	S		R	I	O
G	R	A	M		M	E	N	T	I	O	N	S
			P	L	A	N	S		S	U	E	S
S	M	I	L	E	D		I	C	E	D		
L	A	C	E	S		B	O	R	E	D	O	M
A	D	A		S	C	E	N	E		O	R	E
M	E	N	W	E	R	E		S	W	E	E	T
	D	O	N	E		S	T	O	R	M	S	
I	G	O	R		M	O	U	S	E			
R	O	A	D	M	A	P	S		F	O	R	T
A	L	L		U	T	A	H		U	N	T	O
N	F	L		D	E	L	I		L	E	E	R

PUZZLE 18

S	E	N		D	E	A	D		D	A	R	E
O	N	E		U	R	G	E		E	D	O	M
N	I	H		S	N	A	P		P	A	S	T
	D	E	U	T	E	R	O	N	O	M	Y	
	M	A	Y			S	O	T				
H	A	I	R		D	E	N		S	E	A	
A	S	A		P	O	I	S	E		U	R	N
M	P	H		E	N	D		S	P	A	T	
		A	R	E			V	I	P			
	J	E	S	U	S	T	H	E	S	O	N	
P	E	S	O		T	O	U	R		S	E	A
F	L	A	N		E	G	G	S		E	B	B
C	L	U	E		P	O	S	E		D	O	E

PUZZLE 19

J	E	S	U	S		N		S	E	T	H	
E	V	I	L			O			S	A	U	L
H	E	T	M	A	N		C		T	U	G	
O			B		J	O	S	H		E		
S	A	M	U	E	L		L	I	E	S		S
H		E	L		S	T	A	R				A
A		A	H		S	O		L		I	N	K
P	E	T	E	R		W	V					E
H			A	L		A		A				
A	B	C		C			S	A	R	A	H	S
T		A	C	H	S	A	H		R	A	T	
	T	I	M	E		I	T		V	O	T	E
S	I	N		L	Y	D	I	A		N	E	W

PUZZLE 20

B	R	I	C		C	O	S		C	R	E	E
R	O	S	H		O	R	A		R	A	R	A
A	T	M	O		M	E	D		A	V	I	S
D	E	S	I	R	E		D	I	V	I	N	E
			C	A	L		E	T	A			
C	O	M	E	D	Y		N	A	T	U	R	E
A	R	I								R	A	W
B	R	A	C	E	S		F	A	M	I	N	E
			R	O	T		E	N	E			
R	E	F	U	S	E		E	N	A	B	L	E
O	M	R	I		A	L	B		D	A	I	S
D	U	E	S		M	A	L		O	L	E	O
E	S	T	E		S	B	E		W	I	S	P

PUZZLE 21

L	A	B	S			A	R		S	T	E	W
A	B	I	A		A	B	I		H	A	V	E
K	E	R	C	H	I	E	F		O	N	A	N
E	L	D	A	D		S	L	E	W			
			R		D		E	L	I	S	H	A
C	P	T		R	U	E		I	N	T	E	R
A	L	O	E		E	N	D		G	O	R	E
L	E	A	S	T		D	E	B		P	A	S
F	A	C	T	O	R		F	O	O			
		E	Y	E	S	E	R	V	I	C	E	
R	O	T	E		S	I	N	G	U	L	A	R
I	T	E	M		T	D	D		L	E	N	S
D	O	N	S			S	E		E	A	S	E

PUZZLE 22

M	A	R	S	H	I	L	L		D	R	A	B
A	B	E		U	L	L	A		E	A	S	E
R	A	C	A	L		A	B	R	A	H	A	M
A	S	A	S		M	A	I	D				
H	E	P	S		A	N	N		L	A	P	
			U	S	A			J	A	D	A	
E	D	O	M	I	T	E	S		O	B	A	L
R	A	R	E			O	R	A				
E	N	G		T	O	R		S	T	O	P	
		O	R	C	A			H	O	M	E	
O	B	A	D	I	A	H		B		R	E	T
H	E	R	O		L	A	M	A		A	G	E
S	T	A	R		A	B	I	A	T	H	A	R

PUZZLE 23

C	A	P		E	N	I	D		D	E	L	E
R	N	A		N	I	C	E		E	B	O	N
I	N	S		S	T	E	P		B	R	I	T
B	E	S	T	I	R		I	N	T	O	N	E
		A	G	E		C	O	O				
O	N	I	O	N	S		T	E	R	E	S	H
R	E	L							P	I	E	
B	E	L	O	N	G		D	E	S	I	R	E
		C	A	A		E	R	A				
B	E	T		E	L		V	A	C	A	N	T
E	D	E	R		L	E	I	S		N	O	R
L	I	M	A		O	N	C	E		T	V	A
L	E	A	N		P	O	E	S		S	A	Y

PUZZLE 24

I	N	C	A		S	H	U	A		G	A	S
B	I	R	D		W	E	E	D		A	R	E
I	D	E	A		A	L	L	E	L	U	I	A
D	I	A	M	O	N	D		P	I	L	L	S
		T	A	S		A	T	T				
T	R	U	N	K		O	G			D	A	R
H	U	R	T		T	I	O		P	E	L	E
E	E	E		E	L		C	A	R	O	L	
		A	R	T		R	A	R	I	T	Y	
I	T	H	R	A		B	A	B	A	S		
S	H	E	P	H	E	R	D		B	I	E	R
L	E	A		A	L	I	A		L	O	G	O
E	E	R		B	E	E	R		E	N	O	S

PUZZLE 25

M	E		A	N	T		S	U	M	M	E	R
Y		N	O		G	O		O		R	E	
	J	O	N	A	H		S	T	A	R	S	
B	E		H	O	P	E		H		H		
U	S	A		G	R	A	V	E	N		E	
S	U	R	E		S	A	T		R	A	S	P
	S	E	A	L		Y		A		O	H	
R		R	O	S	E		S		L			
A	P		L	O		R	A	I	N	B	O	W
I	L		I	P		S	A	U	L		A	
S	U	R	E		W	A	S		R	O		G
I	T		S	H	E		S	O	S	O		
N	O		T	R	O	A	S		E	D	E	N

PUZZLE 26

G	O	O	D		B	L	E	S	S	I	N	G
A	N	G	E	R		A	B	L	Y		O	N
T	I	R	E	D		W	O	U	N	D		A
H	O	E	D		U		N	R	A		A	T
E	N	S		O	N	L	Y		G	E	M	
R	S		B	R	I	O		G	O	N	E	
E		A	I		T	R	I		G	E	T	S
R	A	B	B	I		D	R	O	U	G	H	T
	A	B	B	A		L		R	E	L	Y	
E	R	A		M	A	Y	B	E		A	S	K
D	O		P		R		S	M	I	T	E	
E	N	D	U	R	E		I		A	M		E
N		A	T	T	A	I	N	E	D		U	P

PUZZLE 27

A	R	I	S	E		C	O	U	R	A	G	E
G	I	V	E		C	A	L	L		A	L	A
R	B		A	B	I	L	I	T	Y		O	G
E	B	E	R		T	L	V		E	A	R	L
E	O		C	A	Y		E	V	A		Y	E
M	N		H	E		D		A	R	M		
E		B		S	E	O	U	L		A	S	P
N	A	R	R	O	W		N	U	R	S	E	D
T	R	O	U	P	E		P	E	N	T	A	D
	R	A	M		M	A		E	L			
D	O	D	O		P	E	C	K		R	E	D
A	W		U	M	I	A	K		T		D	O
M	S	G	R		A	T		J	O	B		E

PUZZLE 28

T	E	N	D	E	R	H	E	A	R	T	E	D
H	E	A	L		R	A	B	B	I		A	A
A	L	I	V	E		N	B	A		I	C	Y
N		L	Y	I	N	G		S	A	P	H	
K	Y		G	A		S	E	T	H		A	
S	E	A	S	H	O	R	E		M	E	A	L
G	A	D		T	M		V	A		D	A	Y
I	R	O	N		I	T	E	M		E	R	
V		N	E	T		A	N	A	T	I	O	N
I	R	I	J	A	H		Z	O	A	N		
N	O		D	I	A	L		E	P	H		B
G	O	D		L	E	G		D	A		H	E
	M	E		S	T	A	R		Z	E	A	L

PUZZLE 29

```
K I N D N E S S
  L O I N S   P E A C E
K N O W L E D G E   I O N
I O   I   O D   T N T
N   S   G O O D   A H   R
G R A C E   P L O T   S A
D I V I N E   I N   S O N
O D E   C L A N   P I   C
M S   T E M P E R A N C E
    P R   O S     H
  C O U R T   S A V I O R
V I R T U E   L O   S N
I F T H E N   P O W E R
```

PUZZLE 30

```
P I   B R I G H T N E S S
A N H E I R   I H S   P T
  I M A G E   G O   O R
H Q   N H   T H U S   K U
B U R S T   R     M E T
  I E   E C U   C O I N S
E T A   O U T D O   N
X Y L   U P H O L D I N G
P   I S   N T   S O N
R Y E   N A M E   S T O A
E O S   E X C E L L E N T
S K   U S E   E A R   S
S E E K S   C I T Y
```

PUZZLE 31

```
I S R A E L I T E S   H E
N O   P L O D     R U I N
C   G E M   O M R I   R E
U S E S   F L E E   H E M
R   T   D   W E N T   S I
S E   B E G O T T E N   E
    L A B O R     A   A S
P A   S O L S T I C E S
A S H E R A H   T H O U
R I O   A N I   P E N N Y
B L U S H   P E A R   D O
A L S O   A   B Y   H E R
R Y E   S T A B S   A R E
```

PUZZLE 32

```
V I N E Y A R D S   A W E
O F   N E W E R   A N E W
L   G A E L I C     B E
U N D E R   I N L E T S
N O   D   A S K E T H
T R A I T   H   V E R Y
E   N   O   M E R E   E
E L D E R S   O R N E R Y
R A R E R   A D   A   E
  C E L E S T I A L   T
S E W   N O   C   A R E
P   A T R I U M   M E N
A M I D S T   M E L T E D
```

PUZZLE 33

```
A L T A R S   O D I O U S
B O O T   T   N   N U L L
I T   M I M   A N T A E
J U S T I F I E D   I D
A S   U   F L A M   B
H   S A N C T I F I E D
  O S H E A   N E W   A
  M O L E C H   I R E   R
L   L E A K   A S T E R N
A H I   D E N   T I K E
M E T E   D O   E L L   U
P R E E N   S   R E Y E S
S O   N O T E D     H E
```

PUZZLE 34

```
F O U N D   S I N   G O D
I N N   A S H D O D   R E
S C I E N C E   U I   P A
H E T H   A D O R E   A T
E   Y I E L D   I   A H H
R D     P E R S I A
S E L A H   T   H O R E B
  L I V E T H     D O N E
R I C E   E   G R I N D S
O V E N   A L O A N   S E
B E   G A M A L I E L   E
E R R E D   W A S   E   C
  S I R A H   N E R I A H
```

PUZZLE 35

```
B E O R   L O R D   T H E
A N G E R   N A A M   E S
A T   A I   E B R O N A H
L E A D   A   B E D A D
  R A Y   R O I   E A S T
O   R I S E N   I S M   A
F R O N T   E   S T A N D
F I N G E R   O H   N O
I D   W E A P O N   D O
C E P H A S   D O N   A
E R R   R O B E   V O L T
  A N D R E W   A H A H
D A Y   S T E E P   E D S
```

PUZZLE 36

```
M A N N A   N O   E S A U
A S I E L   O N A N   M S
T A S T E   A L L   O N E
T   A S   T H Y   T W O
H E N   F A     A N N A
E R   S E N T   M R   C
W R O T E   A G A G   S T
E B A L   K A D E S H
A D E R   B E L   T H A T
D   Y E A   A N   I K E
L O   U N C L E   M I X
A F F I R M   A M E N
I F   M A S T E R   A G E
```

PUZZLE 37

```
M A I M E D   O W N   I S
O R D E R   I B E A M
M E E T S   S E A P O R T
S N A R E   Y R   A   I
  A L E   B   Y   B U M
W     M E T   A I   B
I D O L S   L O   S T A R
T A P E   J I M   E V E
N I T S   E B B S   A L
E L   S   I V   R A N I
S Y N O D   E V E N   L A
S   N E E D   A D O   T
  S W   N   E D I F Y
```

PUZZLE 38

```
S H A R A R   D A N I E L
A A R O N   A N   G L
V I E   A D O N I J A H
E L T E K E H   S E L A H
  A   I M A G E S   N O
D D S   M A D E   U T A H
R   S   N   S   N A
H O S E A   D E W   T   M
A P   A N   S O D O M
M   S A M   I N A   A X
M A T T H I A S   N A I L
E R A   T S   C R N
R A N   J E H E Z E K E L
```

PUZZLE 39

```
A B L E   N A B   D A R K
S A U L   E G O   E R I E
I S H I   P A N   M A C E
A H I J A H   E N A M E L
  A   E   L E N
E S C H E W   S A D D E N
S E A     A D O
T E M P E R   P A S T O R
  R O E   E   I
O B T A I N   R E S I S T
P R A Y   O G S   E R I A
E I R E   W O O   R A N K
N E A R   N O N   A N G E
```

PUZZLE 40

```
B O B S   S I P   I B R I
A L O T   H E R   N E A R
D E A R   I   O   S A R I
    A I N   F L A M E S
D E V I C E   F U N
E R I T E   J E Z E B E L
E N O   T A R   O V A
D E L I V E R   T E N E T
    N E A   S E V E R E
C R A F T   P E A
R A R A   A P E   D A T E
I C A N   L E A   E D E N
B E N T   A R K   S A N D
```

PUZZLE 41

G	R	A	F		C	R	Y		N	O	E	L
L	A	V	A		H	U	R		O	M	R	I
A	N	I	M		E	H	S		V	E	I	N
D	I	V	I	N	E	R		S	I	N	C	E
			N	O	R		T	I	C			
F	I	R	E		D	E	C	E	A	S	E	
A	N	I		B	R	E	A	K		P	E	N
T	A	B	R	E	T	S			S	P	E	D
			E	S	E		R	A	H			
C	R	A	F	T		R	E	M	O	V	A	L
R	E	T	U		P	O	I		W	E	R	E
A	B	I	S		S	U	N		E	T	N	A
G	A	P	E		I	T	S		R	O	O	F

PUZZLE 42

I	N	N		O	D	O	R		T	R	I	M
R	O	E		B	O	N	E		I	O	T	A
A	V	I		T	R	E	S		F	L	E	W
M	A	N	I	A	C		O	F	F	E	R	S
				I	A		R	I				
O	N	I	O	N	S		T	E	N	D	E	R
N	E	A							U	R	I	
S	T	R	O	N	G		R	E	C	O	R	D
			E	A		E	R					
H	E	A	L	E	R		M	A	T	T	E	R
E	S	L	I		D	I	O	S		A	M	E
L	A	M	E		E	N	T	E		M	I	L
P	U	A	S		N	A	E	S		E	L	Y

PUZZLE 43

B	A	S	E		L	I	E		R	E	D	O
A	L	P	S		A	I	M		A	R	O	D
R	O	U	T		V	I	E		N	A	T	E
B	E	R	A	T	E		R	E	D	S	E	A
			T	A	R		O	R	O			
M	O	S	E	S		A	D	A	M	A	N	T
	R	I		E	L	S		S	I			
P	A	R	A	B	L	E		P	S	A	L	M
			N	R	A		E	R	I			
R	A	N	S	O	M		N	E	M	U	E	L
E	N	O	W		I	N	T		P	R	A	E
A	N	N	E		T	E	E		L	I	V	E
R	O	A	R		E	A	R		E	M	E	

PUZZLE 44

W	A	F	E	R		C	H	A	M	O	I	S
H		O			B	O	A	T		V		N
A	D	D	E	R		T	N	T		E		A
L	A	D	D	E	R		D	I	N	N	E	R
E	T	E	R	N	A	L		R				E
S	E	R	E	D		O	M	E	G	A		
			I	S	H	I		L		N	T	
S	H	E			A	S	S	H	U	R		E
C	A	R	N	A	L		A		T		P	A
R	I	G			L	I	G	H	T		A	C
O	R	O	Z	C	O			O	A	T	H	
L		T	E	A	W	A	G	O	N		H	E
L		N	T		T	O	T	S			S	S

PUZZLE 45

H	O		A	N	N	A		F	I	N	D	
O	M	E	G	A		D	O		E	S	A	U
U	R	I	A	H		A	N		E	R	R	
S	I		G	U	I	D	E		D	A	D	S
E		T	I	M		A	S	A		E		E
	N	O	T		E	H	I		A	L	O	E
H	O	M	E		L		M	I	C		M	K
E	O		S	U	N		U		T		I	
A	N	D		N	A		S	A	I	N	T	S
V		E		N	A	P		G	O		O	
E	G	L	A	I	M		C	A	N	A	A	N
N		A			H	O	P		N	R		
S	A	Y		S	H	E		E	N	T	E	R

PUZZLE 46

S	U	N	D	A	Y		M	A	N		S	W
S	H		M	A		E		O	N	E		
U	N	I	C	O	R	N		D	R	E	A	M
C		N		S	N	O	R	E		A		U
K	I	S	H		A		E	A	R		T	
S		T	O	U	G	H		P	R	I	C	E
	S	A	T		E		F		C	A	R	
F	A	N		A	B	R	A	M		H	O	P
A	N	T		P	A	A	R	A	I		P	A
R	D		P		I		R		A		R	
M	Y	S	I	A		L	O	I	N	S		E
E		O		I	C	E		S		P	A	N
R	U	N		M	A	R	T	H	A		A	T

111

PUZZLE 47

```
B E T H L E H E M ░ A G O
A D A I A H ░ D O C T O R
S ░ T ░ U R ░ P ░ ░ U ░
K G ░ S O D O M ░ S I L K
E A C H ░ D U R A ░ A M ░
T R O O P ░ ░ S I L A S ░
░ L A P ░ J E H O V A H ░
R I C H ░ B I T E ░ U ░
░ C H A R I O T ░ M ░ Z
S ░ E N ░ N E P H E G ░
H A S ░ B A ░ A A R O N
O G ░ B E S O M ░ C L ░
E O N ░ E P H O D ░ Y D
```

PUZZLE 48

```
S E A ░ L O ░ S ░ H O L Y
E R R ░ A N O T H E R ░ E
T E M P T ░ B O A R ░ A
H ░ R E A S O N ░ E A R
░ A ░ R E D D I S H ░
O B E Y ░ E R ░ S T A B
F A ░ E ░ V ░ A H ░ B Y
F A ░ R A G E ░ D I D ░ E
E L I ░ L A ░ O H
R ░ N ░ A D D ░ A B O U T
I T ░ B R I E R ░ U R G E
N A H U M ░ B E O R ░ E N
G N A T ░ T U R N ░ T
```

PUZZLE 49

```
H E A R ░ E L A M ░ D A N
U R ░ E G Y P T ░ A R E A
S ░ A A ░ E ░ E ░ N E O N
H E L P ░ S U M ░ D A N
A S P ░ ░ P P D ░ M ░ I
I C ░ J ░ D O O R ░ S O N
░ A D A M ░ N ░ O K ░ P C
░ P A C E S ░ J O S E P H
H E R O ░ A T O P ░ A H
░ D E B B Y ░ B ░ B R A N
L ░ E I ░ R ░ N O
O N ░ B E N J A M I N ░ N
D O ░ E N G ░ S A M E ░ E
```

PUZZLE 50

```
A B R A H A M ░ I S A A C
N ░ E ░ I D A E ░ O B ░ I
G A B ░ S O D O M ░ I ░ R
E Y E S ░ E ░ O ░ M I C
L ░ K E P I ░ R O E ░ U
░ H A R A N ░ P I L L ░ M
H ░ H E R ░ H ░ A D E ░ C
E R ░ A R A ░ H ░ C C I
R ░ D A N ░ G I ░ H I S
D O ░ T ░ S A R A H ░ E
M ░ L O T ░ R A M ░ H A D
E D ░ N ░ D ░ M A Y
N ░ M E L C H I Z E D E K
```